In Memory Of

Julie Lynch-Letkewicz

Donated By

Her Aunt,

Norma Lynch

3/11

BEAGLE

SMART OWNER'S GUIDE™

FROM THE EDITORS OF  **MAGAZINE**

CONTENTS

Beagle, a Smart Owner's Guide™
part of the Kennel Club Books® Interactive Series™
ISBN: 978-1-593787-72-1 ©2009

Kennel Club Books Inc., 40 Broad St., Freehold, NJ 07728. Printed in China.
All rights reserved. No part of this book may be reproduced in any form,
by Photostat, scanner, microfilm, xerography or any other means, or incorporated
into any information retrieval system, electronic or mechanical,
without the written permission of the copyright owner.

*photographers include Isabelle Francias/BowTie Inc.; Tara Darling/BowTie Inc.; Gina Cioli
and Pamela Hunnicutt/BowTie Inc. Contributing writer: Betty-Anne Stenmark*

For CIP information, see page 176.

If you have taken a Beagle into your home from a responsible breeder or a rescue group — or are planning to do so — congratulations! You have fallen in love with one of the most appealing characters in all of dogdom.

The Beagle's soulful eyes, soft ears, perpetually wagging tail and sweet disposition have made him an American favorite for many decades. Although of English lineage, it was a comic strip in this country that immortalized the breed. Not many dogs can boast of a daily appearance in the newspaper but this lovable hound can, thanks to cartoonist Charles Schulz and *Peanuts*. Yes, Snoopy is a Beagle. Owners can relate to Charlie Brown's occasional exasperation as Snoopy's silly antics know no bounds and keep the neighborhood

kids in stitches. Beagle lovers the world over can't get their fill of Snoopy and appreciate having one of their own.

While exotic, over-the-top breeds ride the wave of popularity, destined to come and go as fickle tastes inevitably change, the Beagle endures. This dog's got staying power. There is nothing dramatic or outrageous about the Beagle's appearance. He is a handy size, portable without being fragile. Being short coated, his grooming needs are easily met with a weekly brushing, along with the nail cutting and ear cleaning that all dogs require. Beagles come in two size varieties — the 13-inch and 15-inch — and several color combinations. The classic tricolor of black, white and tan is most frequently seen but you will also find Beagles in red and white, a lighter shade called lemon and white, and chocolate or blue tricolor (dark brown or blue-gray instead of black, coupled with the usual white and tan trim).

With this Smart Owner's Guide™, you are well on your way to getting your Beagle diploma.

JOIN OUR ONLINE **Club Beagle**™

However, your Beagle education doesn't end here.

You're invited to join **Club Beagle**™ (**DogChannel.com/Club-Beagle**), a FREE online site with lots of fun and instructive features such as:

◆ **forums, blogs** and **profiles** where you can connect with other Beagle owners

◆ **downloadable charts** and **checklists** to help you be a smart and loving Beagle owner

◆ access to Beagle-themed **e-cards** and **wallpapers**

◆ interactive **games**

◆ canine **quizzes**

The **Smart Owner's Guide** series and **Club Beagle** are backed by the experts at DOG FANCY® magazine and DogChannel.com — who have been providing trusted and up-to-date information about dogs and dog people for more than 40 years. Log on and join the club today!

The Beagle's general appearance should remind you of a "miniature Foxhound," according to the American Kennel Club breed standard, and he is "solid and big for his inches, with the wear-and-tear look of the hound that can last in the chase." If you have not seen a Beagle in hunting mode, it is an eye-opener — and an ear-opener, because this breed is vocal in a big way! While the Beagle's quarry is rabbit rather than fox, a pack of these little hounds is relentless, speedy on the chase and joyously baying all the while. He gives new meaning to the phrase "leading by a nose."

Given the breed's history as a scent-hound, a fenced yard is a must. Exercise your Beagle by walking him on a leash or he'll be off to chase the nearest bunny, squirrel or cat. Like all hounds, the Beagle is as stubborn as he is loving, and not very streetwise.

For an owner willing to make a dog a full member of the family, the Beagle is difficult to match. He is loyal, devoted and decid-edly low maintenance. Keep him well exercised but secure, don't let him pack on the pounds, and you'll be enjoying his company for many years to come.

Allan Reznik
Editor-at-Large, DOG FANCY

THE REGAL

BEAGLE

When most dog people think "Beagle," they don't often think "cunning, smart-as-a-fox and twice as naughty," but those big brown eyes and that innocent look can be deceptive. Beagles are laidback, affectionate and can even be a little aloof — but dumb? No way. Still, most Beagle owners agree that the nose is the most intelligent part of their canine pal's anatomy.

"One of Belle's favorite treats is McDonald's Chicken McNuggets, but when we give her a nugget in the car, she buries it under the blanket on the backseat," says Sheila Pinkney of Calgary, Alberta, Canada, about her Beagle, Annabelle. "One time, Belle stole a bun that was in a plastic bag and buried it in the couch. I threw it away, but she went and got it again and buried it in my bed. I found it and threw it away again. We did this four times before I finally took it outside and put it where she wouldn't be able to get it. Once, we found a slice of pizza in the couch, and another time, we found a Boston crème donut."

Though it's not typical of a Beagle to refrain from gulping down a contraband treat

it's a Fact Over the years the Beagle's size has increased, and they now sport the smooth coat we associate with the breed. In America, Beagles come in two distinct size categories, the 13-inch and the 15-inch, while in England they are allowed to be as tall as 16 inches.

Although it has been claimed that Beagles were bred down from Foxhounds, the opposite is true: The larger, quicker Foxhound that accompanied the gentry as they "rode to hounds" on their country estates evolved from a mixture of the Buck Hound and Beagle. Then, as now, the Beagle was the working man's dog, and farmers in England and Ireland continue to hunt with their Beagle packs today.

before his owner even knows he has it. This wacky behavior is indicative of what makes the breed so charming; it's unpredictability and determination. How else is that rabbit going to get caught? Read on to discover what life is really like with the loveable Beagle.

PUPPY POWER

A Beagle's energy level generally changes as the dog ages. Beagle puppies are full of vigor, always ready for an exhausting romp. Teenage and adult Beagles have a lot of stamina; after all, they're bred for hunting and chasing game. Older Beagles can fatigue easily, but that's true of nearly every breed.

"Buster and Rocky have energy spurts where they'll play really hard," says Marnie Burge of Pittsburgh, Pa., of her two Beagle puppies. "After about 10 minutes, they're pooped. They sleep well through the night and have their play time before we leave for work. They like to wrestle and play keep-away. We give each puppy the exact same bone, but they'll fight over them just to play."

Ginny Butterfield, a Beagle owner from Cranberry Township, Pa., says her two

Beagles are on opposite sides of energy-level extremes. "George likes to eat and sleep," Butterfield says. "We need to wake him up to go outside. GiGi, on the other hand, is always playing, romping and performing like a circus dog."

Beagles, like many other breeds, tend to take on the energy level of their household, according to Bruce Cornely, a writer from Gainesville, Fla. "I'm a quiet, homebody type, and my Beagles are like that as well," he says. "They've always been house dogs and only enjoy being outside for short periods of time. They're content to be sacked out on the sofa or my bed. They're surprisingly adaptable."

DETERMINED DOGS

OK, the nose itself isn't stubborn, but it's behind some of the Beagle's seemingly stubborn behavior. Once a Beagle happens upon a scent, you'll be hard-pressed to regain his interest in anything else.

"My husband once chased [our Beagle] Shelley for five miles through the woods after she got on the scent of a deer," says Alice Moser of Shavertown, Pa. "She screeched and howled the entire time, so it wasn't hard for him to follow her, but she would not come to him, no matter how many times he called her. She was focused solely on that scent. That was the last time she was let off the leash outside the confines of our fenced yard!"

Be careful any time your Beagle is roaming freely. Not only do Beagles enjoy taking off after wild game, they're bred to be followed by their human companions; in other words, running after the dog only fuels the chase.

"I was working with Bosco on coming in a huge park, off leash," says Kim Caporale of Homewood, Ill., about her 2-year-old Beagle. "He was doing great, when all of a

Warning! Beagles can be addictive. If you have one, you might find yourself wanting more.

Meet other Beagle owners just like you. On our Beagle forums, you can chat about your Beagle and ask other owners for advice on training, health issues and anything else about your favorite dog breed. Log onto **DogChannel.com/Club-Beagle** for details!

Beagles are a breed built around a nose!

sudden a flock of geese landed in the park. He took off so fast that I thought I'd never see him again, but he eventually came back. It's extremcly difficult to train Beagles outdoors when their main focus is sniffing for squirrels and rabbits."

Most Beagle owners soon learn that their dogs not only can't be trusted off leash, but Beagles are also drawn to escaping the house or yard to track game. "Chester is an escape artist; he'll dart out the door at the first sign of another dog or a squirrel," says Marta Kane of Massapequa Park, N.Y. "When their nose leads them on a hunting trail, it's often difficult to divert their attention."

The nose also leads to thievery. A new Beagle owner soon learns to put food away quickly. "If you have a sandwich in your hand and you're not paying attention, that sandwich will be gone," Pinkney says. "Don't be persuaded by their sweet faces. I call [my Beagle] Belle 'the Queen of the Mile;' if you give her an inch, she'll take a mile."

TRAINING IS A MUST

You have to take a kind of Zen outlook on training a Beagle. If you want your

Younger Beagles have loads of energy, but they mellow out a bit as they get older.

Beagle's attention, you have to be more exciting and more rewarding than the proverbial rabbit (or squirrel or sandwich, whatever the case).

"Training a Beagle can be a challenge to the novice trainer," says Carol Herr, a professional handler and Beagle breeder from Summerfield, Fla. "They think all the time, and they get bored easily, but most trainers think they're just being stubborn. I find that they're no more stubborn than any other breed. Sometimes their noses get them into trouble, but because they're so food motivated, you can train them to respond to food. That's why all my Beagles think their middle name is 'cookie.'"

All of Denise Nord's Beagles are clicker-trained. Nord, a certified dog trainer and owner of Canine Connection Dog Training in Rogers, Minn., says that her dogs love to work. Her two oldest Beagles were the first — and maybe the only — Beagles titled in conformation, obedience, agility, tracking and rally.

"All of my training is based on positive motivation and reward," Nord says. "Beagles are extremely intelligent and quick to learn, but you have to make it worth their while. If it isn't fun and rewarding from the dog's point of view, the dog isn't going to play the game."

A TRUE CHOWHOUND

Unlike some breeds, such as Labrador Retrievers and Golden Retrievers, the Beagle wasn't bred to find his human pack. Instead, he was bred to track game and follow his nose. So, you'll have to go the extra mile to keep your dog concentrating on training lessons.

"You must have very smelly treats to train your Beagle so he will focus on you," says Nicki Puckett of Virginia Beach, Va. "If you

can convince your Beagle that you're the bearer of good, smelly things, you can convince him to do almost anything for you. Beagles are noses with legs."

Kathleen Weaver of Farmers Branch, Texas, says she doesn't think Beagles are the most highly trainable dogs, but she has a theory for that. "It took me several years and someone else to point this out, but in order to find rabbits, Beagles have to be able to generate random behavior," she says. "This gets in the way when you're trying to train them for obedience and agility. Few breeds need this randomness, and it does make training more difficult. I can work on a behavior for many repetitions, but suddenly I'll get a completely different behavior. You don't see that in other breeds as much."

The key to training a Beagle correctly is to find the right trainer who will use the right training method with your dog. Someone who doesn't understand Beagles might misunderstand their behavior.

"I've found that not every trainer understands Beagles," says Teresa Locatelli, a

NOTABLE & QUOTABLE

The Beagle is a very loving, good house pet — if by the time they are 3 months old, you do some form of obedience training. If you don't, they become very dominant dogs.

— tracking judge Carole Bolan of Groton, Mass.

Beagle owner from Soquel, Calif. "Roo and I were sent to a time-out area by ourselves and made to leave an agility class because he was barking. An excited Beagle barks and shouldn't be punished for having fun on a non-competitive agility course."

Even though training might be challenging, don't mistake that for lack of brain power. The Beagle is no dummy. "I've long suspected that Jenny is capable of figuring things out and thinking for herself," says John Thompson of Battle Creek, Mich. "Once, I was lying on the couch and watching TV when she went to the door like she wanted out. I got up to let her out, but she ran over to the couch and jumped up on it instead. She had stolen my seat."

BOYS AND THEIR BEAGLES

A big upside to owning a Beagle is the breed's high tolerance for children and their antics. This family-oriented breed takes nearly everything a kid can dish out. "Beagles are wonderful with children," Herr says. "It has often been said, 'All little boys should have a Beagle as a pet.' The only thing I worry about with small children is a

Beagle puppy getting up in their faces, because Beagle puppies have a tendency to lick a lot. Beagles also have soft, fairly long ears that seem to have an attraction for young children, so children need to learn not to pull on the ears."

If you have kids, remind them that any food in their hands is fair game for the chowhound in their life. A small child might become upset if your dog steals his or her treat. Conversely, teach the child not to take

On average, Beagles range from about 20 to 30 pounds. Although the breed is refreshingly free of health problems, they have an insatiable appetite and an accompanying tendency toward obesity. Often quite content to sit beside you watching TV for hours on end, Beagles were bred to be active outdoor dogs and daily exercise is required to keep them fit and handsome.

it's a **Fact**

Every child deserves to grow up with a dog, and there might not be a better breed than a Beagle!

things away from the dog, and to be gentle and compassionate with him.

"My two Beagles are wonderful with kids," says Ursula E. Lehman of Hudson, Ohio. "Blade was a pup when my godchild, Karlie, was just a few months old, and he would pop over to her and just love her to pieces with kisses galore. He would tolerate her pulling his ears and tail. As she got older, he had to tolerate even more."

The Beagle's temperament is legendary, and his reputation is made of more fact than fiction: This breed really is a great family member and a loving companion. Sure, his obedience skills might leave something to be desired, but many people have managed to put obedience and agility titles onto their Beagles. All this breed needs is a patient owner with a handful of liver snacks.

OH, AND ABOUT THAT NOSE

If the weirdest thing your Beagle has ever eaten is half a cantaloupe, rejoice. A Beagle's voracious appetite — driven by his incredibly sensitive nose — can be not only bizarre, but it also can be downright dangerous. In addition, the lengths they'll go to in order to nab a sniffed-out item boggle the mere human mind. Here are a few of the more unusual culinary experiences of Beagles shared by owners and friends of owners around the country.

"One of mine ate a pencil once, metal piece and all," Nord says. Luckily, it passed through with no problem. As did the loaf of bread eaten by a Beagle belonging to a friend of Sue Pearson of Iowa City, Iowa. That crafty pooch had to learn to open a kitchen drawer to satisfy his craving. Many a show Beagle has shown his persistence by eventually eating through an owner's pocket to get to stashed treats.

Fairly benign and even funny stuff so far, right? Not so of the tampon that a Beagle once ate. "Fortunately she didn't have to have surgery, but she got very ill," Nord says of her friend's dog.

Many owners report having dogs that discovered a not-so-well-hidden stash of dog food only to eat to the point that their stomachs looked like basketballs. Three of Janiece Harrison's Beagles once found their way into what must have seemed like doggie heaven: "Daisy, Sadie and Bo once raided the refrigerator," she said. "We don't crate the dogs while we're gone and we have a dog door. The first thing I noticed when we got home that day was plastic wrap out in the yard. I went in and there were two or three Tupperware containers spread around the den. The dogs clearly just got in there and had a big smorgasbord."

Their individual reactions were humorous. "Daisy and Sadie were pretty old by then," Harrison recalls. "Daisy was just lying on her dog bed with this look on her face like if she could smoke a cigarette she'd be doing it. Sadie, who was really, really sweet, ran to the refrigerator as if to show us that there was this special place she had discovered and she would share. Poor Bo was just a pup, and I'm afraid the main thing he'd been hearing for much of his life was 'Bo, no!' The

Beagles are a long-lived breed, so acquiring one can mean a commitment of 13 years or more. In their senior years, nothing is sweeter than their graying faces, which become even softer and seem to take on the calmness and wisdom of beloved elders.

NOTABLE & QUOTABLE

Beagles are stubborn, energetic pack animals who need a lot of human contact. They like being in contact with you or another dog. They see you as their pack. They aren't couch decorations. They want and need interaction.
— Linda Forrest, founder of SOS Beagle Rescue Inc. in Bordentown, N.J.

second we walked through the door, he hit the floor as if to say, 'Oh, I'm sorry.'"

This half-funny/half-frightening experience taught the Harrisons to always be sure the refrigerator is closed tight.

"The best and worst thing about Beagles is how food driven they are," Pearson says. "It makes them easy to train. It makes them attentive during training. But they are also driven by their nose and appetite. If you let them, I think Beagles would eat until they popped. They really are insatiable."

A Beagle's strange appetites might make for great stories, but through the laughter, every Beagle owner knows they need to protect their dogs from themselves by diligently keeping edibles out of reach.

RAINBOW OF COLORS

Like most hounds, Beagles come in a rich variety of colors. The most common is tricolor, featuring a black saddle with white legs, chest and belly and a tan color on the head and around the saddle edges. Many also have a white blaze on the face. Tricolor pups are born black and white with the tan devcloping as they grow older.

On the other hand, the red-and-white Beagle has no black at all. The red ranges from a light tan to a darker rust. These pups are born with red and white coloring, or sometimes, they are solid white, with their pigment emerging later.

Lemon and whites — the lemon varying from an off-white to a darker yellow — are often born completely white. Black and whites, sometimes having a gray saddle, are comparatively rare. Solid liver is not a recognized color.

Whatever color a Beagle is, he can also have freckling, mottling, ticking or grizzling. Another commonality: All Beagles should have their signature white-tipped tail, or

"stern" as it's referred to in hound parlance. Along with their throaty, musical cry known as "baying," the Beagles' joyful little flags waving excitedly above their rumps signal the hunters of their whereabouts in the field.

According to the American Kennel Club Beagle breed standard (a written description of what an ideal Beagle should look like), a tail that is too long, too curved forward or backward, has a "teapot" curve, or is without sufficient coat or brush, dubbed a "rat tail," constitutes a fault. As part of their regular grooming regimen, Beagles have their tails gently blunted and rounded at the tip only, usually with thinning shears. Set moderately high, the tail is carried gaily — but not turned forward over the back — and features a distinctive brush on its underside, which is not trimmed.

Beagles are the perfect sized dog: not too small to be fragile and not to big that you can't plop them in your lap!

Parr for the Course

Ellen Parr knows firsthand how a little TLC can transform a dog others might have disregarded. One of her Beagles, adopted from the humane society in Woodburn, Ore., was a female named Pippi that had been abandoned because she kept escaping. When Parr, a member of the local breed club, got the call, she and her husband immediately went to pick up the dog.

"She was skin and bones, flea-infested with hot spots and a big wound on her back," she says. "We looked at each other, looked into her eyes and she was ours. But when we got her home and cleaned her up, we discovered that she was very much afraid of women and much preferred my husband's company. She was also afraid of brooms and the pooper scooper. Plus, if you moved your feet very quickly she was terrified. We assumed that she hadn't been treated well at all, likely by the woman who had owned her previously."

Even in the loving care of Parr and her husband, Pippi exhibited an on-again, off-again lameness. Upon closer examination, the Parrs discovered it was probably caused by a pellet lodged near Pippi's spine.

That hasn't stopped Pippi from settling in, and now, Pippi rules the roost.

"This brave girl has blossomed into a wonderful dog," Parr says. "We have plans to start working on training her as a therapy dog, since she is the best cuddler in the whole world, and her soft face and oh-so-expressive eyes can melt anyone's heart. She's never once tried to escape from us either. I guess when you know you have it good, you've got no reason to leave."

For anyone who has loved a Beagle, it may be difficult to understand how anyone could give one up, but hundreds of Beagles are in need of loving homes. If you are considering bringing a Beagle into your family, Beagle rescue workers across the country urge you to consider adopting a rescue Beagle.

"Beagles have so much love and laughter to give, it's certainly worth giving them a second chance," Parr says. "I cherish every day with my dogs because they give so much to me."

Perhaps a Beagle is out there, somewhere, waiting to add love and laughter to your life, too.

THE BEAGLE BULLETIN

This small hound has a great big personality.

COUNTRY OF ORIGIN: Great Britain

WHAT HIS FRIENDS CALL HIM: Snoopy, Slick, Houndini, Bugle, Wags

SIZE: two varieties: 13 inches and under, or up to 15 inches; typical weight is 20 to 30 pounds.

COAT & COLOR: Any hound color, common colors include black, tan and white; red and white; and pale tan and white. The feet and tail tip should be white.

PERSONALITY TRAITS: Good natured and independent, this outgoing and friendly dog gets along with almost everyone.

WITH KIDS: Beagles are great child companions.

WITH OTHER PETS: This breed gets along well with other pets (rabbits, though, not so much!)

ENERGY LEVEL: moderate/low

EXERCISE NEEDS: This breed's exercise needs are moderate; regular walks and playtime will suffice.

GROOMING NEEDS: Beagles don't need much beyond regular brushing and baths; be sure to clean their ears often to prevent infections.

TRAINING NEEDS: These dogs do well with learning basic training techniques, but it may take a few training sessions to catch on.

LIVING ENVIRONMENT: Beagles can live anywhere from an apartment to a house with a yard.

LIFESPAN: 12 to 13 years

HISTORY

O edipus had one with legendary hunting prowess named Argon, who lived to the ripe old age of 20, waiting for his master's return. The ancient Spartans had them, and prized them so much that they immortalized them in marble sculpture. Sir Gawain, one of the knights of King Arthur's round table, had one beside him on his noble crusade searching for the Holy Grail. Geoffrey Chaucer probably had one, as he empathetically describes the Prioress in his *Canterbury Tales* weeping at the death of her "smalle houndes." And Queen Elizabeth I prized hers for their lovely voices, compact size and persistence during the hunt.

Were all these dogs Beagles? The same soft-eyed, floppy-eared, scent-obsessed Beagles we know and adore today? Not exactly. The name "Beagle" wasn't even standard until the 19th century, but small hunting hounds with melodious voices, keen noses and the ability to follow a scent trail are the ancestors to our modern Beagles. In addition, small scenthounds have lived and worked beside humankind for thousands of years, distinguishing themselves time and

Did You Know? **Cartoonist Charles Schulz created the *Peanuts* comic strip,** which was based largely on a Beagle named Snoopy who "dispensed more wisdom than any adult." Schulz was awarded, by resolution, a Congressional Gold Medal, in 2000.

again as happy companions, energetic hunters and persistent (sometimes to a fault) when it comes to tracking a scent. Let's take a closer look at how small pack hounds evolved through the ages to produce that dark-eyed, velvet-eared fellow, baying at the squirrels in your yard.

COMMON SCENTS

Scenthounds have always come in different sizes, from the leggy Bloodhound to the smallest Beagle, each serving various functions and excelling at different kinds of hunting. "It's difficult to trace an accurate history of the Beagle prior to 1800 because writers used the terms Beagle, Harrier and Foxhound indiscriminately," says Beagle historian and breeder, Dr. Charles A. Kitchell, of Eldridge, Iowa. "The three hound types were also frequently interbred to suit personal preferences, and to adapt to variations in local terrain."

In other words, scenthounds were big, small and everything in between, but specific breeds were hardly defined. Somewhere in the mix, the ancestors of the Beagle sniffed merrily along after rabbits.

Beagles probably descended from the smallest of these hounds, custom-designed for those less interested in the fast-paced fox hunt and more interested in chasing hare and rabbits. The smaller hounds had noses keen enough to follow the intricate ins and outs of rabbit and hare trails, and voices loud enough to call a hunter from miles away, baying the Beagle equivalent of, "I found 'em! Come and get 'em!"

ON THE CONTINENT

Ubiquitous in Britain, where the Beagle was officially born, small hounds also found their way to many other European countries, or arose in other locations independently, including Italy and especially France. "England is usually given credit as the birthplace of the Beagle. However, France should be given more credit for its influences on the development of the present hound," Kitchell says. French imports to England did indeed influence the look of the modern Beagle, giving it a broader muzzle, a lower voice and keener scenting ability, Kitchell says.

If you were to travel back in time to 17th century England and gather a pack of these small British hounds, you would wonder if they were related at all. From Southern Hounds descended from French imports via William the Conqueror, to the lighter-boned, faster-moving North Country Beagles native to Britain, small hounds were anything but standardized in their looks.

But as the aristocracy became more interested in fox hunting and less interested in the slower, smaller hounds, Beagles did become more standardized for one purpose:

it's a Fact

In 1792, _Sporting Magazine_ printed the following: "Of those dogs who are kept for the business of the chase in this country, the [B]eagle is the smallest, and is only used in hunting the hare. Though far inferior in point of speed to that animal, he follows by the exquisiteness of his scent, and traces her footsteps through all her various windings with great exactness and perseverance. His tones are soft and musical, and add greatly to the pleasures of the chase."

Despite his humble looks and demeanor, the Beagle has a legacy rooted in the upper echelons of society reaching all the way back to ancient Greece.

The Beagle is reputed to be the best scent hound in his group.

securing dinner. Small hounds were perfect for the peasantry, who couldn't afford the time or expense of fox hunting, but still needed a dog who could be a valuable resource, which they could keep easily and cheaply inside with the family. You didn't need a horse to follow a Beagle, so you could hunt with them on foot. Scoring a big juicy hare or rabbit meant dinner on the table, so even when the aristocracy's whims turned elsewhere, small hounds were in no danger of dying out.

"Farmers owned Beagles and used them to hunt for the family meal. Rabbit was a common food source back then, and the instinct to hunt rabbit was much more useful for a family needing dinner on the table than the instinct to hunt fox," says Ruth Darlene Stewart, a Beagle breeder in Theodore, Ala.

In the 1830s, Rev. Phillip Honeywood of Essex actively bred large packs of hounds for their superior hunting ability, and the Beagle's prowess as a competitor blossomed, and commoners learned the allure of the field trial. The Beagle added organized competition to his repertoire of skills. Beagles had already begun to win favor again with the aristocracy — British royalty from Queen Elizabeth I onward had hunted with small hounds — but Honeywood brought the sport to the masses. Clubs formed devoted to field trials and other hunting activities.

As the Beagle became more uniform in regards to his appearance, the name became more consistently applied. In 1873, Britain's Kennel Club officially recognized the Beagle by name, and in 1891, the Association of Masters of Harriers and Beagles formed in England to separate Beagles and Harriers and list each in their own stud books. "For the first time, interbreeding between Beagles and Harriers was officially discouraged in England," Kitchell says. The name "Beagle" finally began to mean something particular and specific.

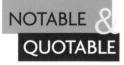

Beagles are a hunting breed, and their world revolves around their incredible sense of smell. This often gets them into trouble, especially with a novice owner. You need to engage that nose to successfully live with a Beagle.

— Denise Nord of Rogers, Minn., founder of Beagle Obedience Network Excellent

Hunters are able to discern their Beagle's progress while tracking a scent based on the way the dog's tail wags.

ACROSS THE POND

In America, small hounds were nothing new, even when the AKC officially recognized the Beagle in 1884. "Hounds of various sizes, colors and descriptions probably sailed to America with the earliest immigrants," Kitchell says. But these early hounds didn't much resemble our beautiful clear-coated, straight-legged Beagles. Many were crossed with Basset Hounds and Dachshunds, and possibly had terrier influences, too. They varied in appearance with longer muzzles, lighter bones and decorated with mottling and ticking. They weren't always pretty, but they were quick, full of energy and good in the field.

The influence of these early American Beagles is more evident in field Beagles than in show Beagles today, which more closely resemble the English Foxhound in miniature (as the breed standard states they should). "Most of the Beagles registered today are bred for field, not show. The National Beagle Club was formed in 1887 by people who hunted, and the club sponsored field events long before it sponsored dog shows," says John Shaw, a Beagle breeder in Walnut Hill, Ill., and an active member of the NBC.

it's a Fact

In early times, the British hound predecessors were split into two classes: the "Buck Hound," a larger variety that hunted deer, and the smaller Beagles that hunted hare. During the 18th century, fox hunting on horseback became more popular with the British royalty and upper classes than trailing the hounds on foot while they puzzled in endless circles on the trail of a hare.

A Band of Brothers

Once upon a time, scenthounds were all interbred and mixed up. Even now that breeds have distinguishing characteristics and individual names, it's easy to see some similarities in these scenthound cousins. Here is a guide to the Beagle's brothers:

Basset Hound: Hailing from France and descended from the famous French St. Hubert Hounds, the Basset Hound looks like a larger, lower, stockier Beagle, or a Bloodhound on short legs.

Bloodhound: Of French descent and probably just as ancient as the Beagle, the long-legged Bloodhound has a similar tail, long ears and wide-open nose. However, the Bloodhound is much larger, droopier and louder than the Beagle.

Dachshunds: Dachsies may have been occasionally crossbred with Beagles, but today's wiener dog looks nothing like the Beagle.

American Foxhound: A more recent breed than the Beagle, the American Foxhound evolved from taller hunting hounds who came to America with the colonists in the 17th century. Also a proficient field-trialer, the American Foxhound is better suited than the Beagle to hunt fox in packs at high speed while the hunter follows on horseback.

English Foxhound: The Beagle breed standard says the Beagle should look like "a foxhound in miniature form." But that doesn't mean the English Foxhound came first. In a debate reminiscent of the chicken and the egg, historians disagree about who was bred down, or up, from whom. Although the English Foxhound does resemble a larger, taller, faster version of the Beagle, many believe the Beagle came first and the Foxhound was bred with other hounds to increase his size and speed.

Harrier: Closely related to the Beagle up until the 19th century when the two breeds officially diverged, the Harrier looks like a larger Beagle. The Harrier may have evolved from French hunting hounds and perhaps some sighthounds, but today it excels at hunting hare (which are larger and faster than rabbits), or hunting fox at a slower pace while the hunter follows on foot. The Harrier may have been bred down from the Foxhound, which may have been bred up from the Beagle, but nobody knows for sure.

Where did the name come from? The word "Beagle" probably comes from the Old French *bee gueule*, meaning "gaping gullet," a reference to the Beagle's ability to make a lot of noise. Others guess that the name is derived from the Old English *begel*, the French *beigh* or the Celtic *beag*, which all translate to "small."

"The national club's emphasis has always been on hunting, and the breed standard is specifically written to emphasize function in the field," adds Shaw's wife Peggy. "The original purpose of the Beagle has always been in the field. Even today in the NBC, the primary members have formal Beagle packs for hunting. The supporting members are the people who show their Beagles in conformation."

THE MODERN BEAGLE

Today, Beagles bred for field and for show have diverged significantly. "If you look at a show Beagle next to a field Beagle, they look like two separate breeds," Shaw says. "Field people are interested almost entirely in performance. Show people are more interested in what the breed looks like." Although Shaw admits that there are always exceptions, he observes that show dogs generally have heavier bones, shorter backs and squarer muzzles. "Field dogs have a somewhat snipier [more pointed] muzzle and shorter ears, while show dogs have longer ears and more level toplines [the line in profile from shoulder to tail]. Field people don't care about the topline as long as the dog runs the rabbit right," Shaw says.

In 50 years, there has been only a single dual champion — a dog who earns the title of Champion in field trials as well as the show ring. "There isn't a lot of cross-over. A few people are trying to produce dogs who can do both, but most Beagle breeders are more interested in one type or the other," says Peggy Shaw. "That's the nature of the breed right now."

As the Beagle became more fully defined and minutely refined in America, the breed also became classified into two sizes: 13-inch and 15-inch (the British standard doesn't separate the sizes). The size variation came about because of differing hunting terrain and the differing size of the rabbits. When you're hunting in wide-open spaces with less underbrush, as in the desert or the Midwest, and you are hunting jack rabbits, the 15-inch dog keeps up better. But try putting a larger dog in a really thick briar patch or sending him down hollows and logs and holes. A smaller Beagle will out-do a larger Beagle in thickets with the smaller cottontail rabbits, but most packs contain both sizes so there's a Beagle best suited to every situation.

A NOBLE NOSE

The Beagle's noble origins are still reflected in the Beagle we know today. Among her 12 Beagles, all bred for the show ring, breeder Ruth Darlene Stewart from Theodore, Ala., says that about half of them bark, bay and worry about the squirrels in the trees in her yard, while the other half lie on the porch looking down their noses at the vermin with little interest. "The ones who retain that instinct, scream and bay for hours, making all kinds of racket. It's a good thing I live in the country where people are more tolerant of that kind of thing," Stewart says. "Beagles are designed to be vocal so the hunter can find them when they wander ahead. It's something pet owners have to be prepared for."

You have an unbreakable bond with your dog, but do you always understand him? Go online and download "Dog Speak," which outlines how dogs communicate. Find out what your Beagle is saying when he barks, howls or growls. Go to **DogChannel.com/Club-Beagle** and click on "Downloads."

The instinct to range far ahead still lives in the modern Beagle. "Whereas sporting dogs are bred to stay within a certain area so they can hear their handler's whistle, Beagles don't do that. There is a disconnect between the nose and the ear when they get the scent. Don't expect them to stay on any hiking trail," Stewart warns. "The world has changed, but the Beagle hasn't; in this age of traffic, property lines, theft and other dangers, you can't let a pet Beagle go off leash."

A HUNTING HERITAGE

The Beagle is still bred and built for hunting, although which qualities contribute best to the sport is still a matter of debate. Most agree that the Beagle should have a durable, protective coat and a flag on the tail to withstand the impact of brush in the field, but not everybody agrees those long Beagle ears.

"Field people tend to breed for a shorter ear so they don't get torn up out in the field," Peggy Shaw says. "But show people have kept the ear long, preferring it to come out to the end of the nose, based on the theory that the length of ear helps funnel scent into the nose. That function is debat-able, but that is the origin of the long ear."

According to Stewart, overall structure is among the most basic aspects of the breed standard, and the most influential for function. "The most vague and the most critical is certainly structure, or how the bones should be put together," she says. "A dog with nice straight legs and a good amount of bone will hold up in the field better than a dog with crooked legs and not a lot of bone. A dog with a body that is too long will have back problems as well as problems running. A dog who is short won't have the flexibility to get in and around after the rabbit, so it's all based on the ability to move, flex, bring in the scent; in other words, it's all about function."

Despite varying interpretations, this is the heart and soul of the written standard. "Every bit of the written breed standard, as vague and open to interpretation as it may be, addresses the need to hunt, not the need to sit on the couch," Stewart adds.

ONE BEAGLE, TWO BEAGLE ...

Traditionally hunted in packs or braces (pairs), Beagles have retained a strong instinct to be part of a pack, which is why he must be included in the family. "These aren't solitary animals," Stewart says. "They were bred for many centuries to be part of a pack. Whether it's a human pack or a dog pack, the Beagle needs to be involved."

Knowing the Beagle's long history will help owners better understand the needs, instincts and drives of this challenging but charming little hound. The next time your Beagle is dashing nose-to-the-ground across the yard with no indication that he hears you, you'll know why. When your Beagle pesters you for some attention, action and a challenging game just so he can feel a part of the pack, you'll know why. It's simply the Beagle way.

Did You Know?

Beagles were extremely popular with the British monarchy. In the 14th and 15th centuries, both King Edward II and King Henry VII kept packs of "glove Beagles," so named because they were tiny enough to fit on a glove. A bit larger were the "pocket Beagles," who were carried to the field in the hunter's jacket. Wire-haired varieties were also quite common. By the time Elizabeth I took the throne in 1558, nearly every member of the gentry kept a pack of hounds.

BEAGLES AND

BREEDERS

As rough and tumble as the Beagle can be, nothing is cuter than a Beagle puppy. His sweet face and round little body inspire *oohs* and *ahhs* from all who see him. That wonderful endearing quality, however, can also distract you from taking the time and doing the legwork necessary to find a puppy who's not only adorable but also healthy in body and temperament. The key to finding the best Beagle puppy for you is to resist being charmed into a hasty decision and instead wait to find a responsible breeder. Then, you can have fun picking just the right puppy from a litter of lovable sweet faces.

You're going to have your Beagle for more than 12 years, so the time you spend early on to locate a healthy, well-adjusted puppy from a reputable breeder will definitely pay off in the long run. Look for a dedicated and ethical breeder who values good health and stable personalities, and who really cares what happens to the dog for the rest of his life.

Why is this so important? This is a breed with a unique personality who needs to be bred correctly by someone with experience

it's a Fact

Local referrals are essential. A breeder who belongs to a local Beagle club shows active involvement in the breed and breeds according to that particular club's code of ethics. That's who you want to do business with: a breeder who abides by a code of ethics.

and really knows what he or she is doing. If not, you may wind up with a dog who's overly aggressive, has a ton of health problems and doesn't even look like a Beagle.

Be sure to avoid puppy mills and backyard breeders. Puppy mills are large-scale breeding operations that produce puppies in an assembly-line fashion without regard to health and socialization. Backyard breeders are typically well-meaning, regular pet owners who simply do not possess enough knowledge about the breed and breeding to produce healthy puppies.

The American Kennel Club and the United Kennel Club provide a list of breeders in good standing with their organizations. See *Resources*, chapter 13, on page 166 for contact information.

EVALUATING BREEDERS

Once you have the names and numbers of breeders in your area, start contacting them to find out more about their breeding programs. But, before you contact them, prepare some questions to ask that will elicit the information you need to know.

Prospective buyers interview breeders in much the same way that a breeder should interview a buyer. Make a list of questions and record the answers so you can compare them to the answers from other breeders whom you may interview later. The right questions are those that help you identify who has been involved with the breed for a respectable number of years and who is actively showing their dogs. Ask in-depth questions regarding the genetic health of the parents, grandparents and great grandparents of any puppy you are considering. Ask what sort of genetic testing program the breeder adheres to.

You should look to see if a breeder actively shows his or her dogs in conformation events (aka dog shows). Showing indicates that the breeder is bringing out examples from his or her breeding program for the public to see. If there are any obvious problems, such as temperament or general conformation, they will be readily apparent. Also, the main reason to breed Beagles is to improve the quality of the breed. If the breeder is not showing, then he or she is more likely to be breeding purely for the monetary aspect and may have less concern for the welfare and future of the breed.

Inquiring about health and determining the breeder's willingness to work with you in the future are also important for the potential puppy buyer to learn. The prospective buyer should see what kind of health guarantees the breeder gives. Find out if the breeder will be available for future consultation regarding your Beagle, and if the breeder will take your dog back if something unforeseen happens.

Prospective buyers should ask plenty of questions, and in return, buyers should also be prepared to answer questions posed by a responsible breeder who wants to make sure his or her puppy is going to a good home. Be prepared for a battery of questions from the breeder regarding your purpose for wanting a Beagle and whether

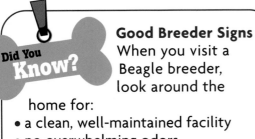

Did You Know?

Good Breeder Signs When you visit a Beagle breeder, look around the home for:
- a clean, well-maintained facility
- no overwhelming odors
- an overall impression of cleanliness
- socialized dogs and puppies

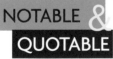
NOTABLE & QUOTABLE

Epilepsy in Beagles is very common. I see more of it in the rescues that come through here from breeders who just breed a male to a female and know nothing of the dogs' backgrounds. Reputable breeders are going to have the dog's eyes checked. They're going to see if there are any thyroid problems. Reputable breeders look for these health problems, and they try to breed away from them.

— *Beagle breeder Ruth Darlene Stewart from Theodore, Ala.*

you can properly care for one. Avoid buying from a breeder who does little or no screening. If a breeder doesn't ask any questions, they are not concerned with where their pups end up. In this case, the dogs' best interests are probably not the breeder's motive for breeding.

The buyer should find a breeder who is willing to answer any questions they have and are knowledgeable about the history of the breed, health issues and the background of their own dogs. Learn about a breeder's long-term commitment to the Beagle breed and to his or her puppies after they leave the kennel.

Look for breeders who know their purpose for producing a particular litter, those who are knowledgeable in the pedigrees of their dogs and of the Beagle breed itself, and have had the necessary health screenings performed on the parents. They should also ask you for references to show that they are interested in establishing a relationship with you in consideration for a puppy. If after one phone conversation with a breeder, the person is supplying you with an address in which to send a deposit, continue your search for a reputable breeder elsewhere.

CHOOSING THE RIGHT PUP

Once you have found a breeder you are comfortable with, your next step is to pick the right puppy. The good news is that if you have done your homework and found a responsible breeder, you can count on this person to give you plenty of help in choosing the right pup for your personality and lifestyle. In fact, most good breeders will recommend a specific puppy once they know what kind of dog you want.

After you have narrowed down the search and selected a reputable breeder, rely on the experience of the breeder to help you select your puppy. The selection of the puppy depends a lot on what purpose the pup is being purchased for. If the pup is being purchased as a show prospect, the breeder will offer his or her assessment of the pups that meet this criteria and will be able to explain the strengths and faults of each pup.

Whether your Beagle puppy is show or pet quality, a good, stable temperament is vital for a happy relationship. Generally, you want to avoid a timid puppy or a very dominant one. Temperament is very important, and a reputable breeder should spend a lot of time with the pups and be able to offer an evaluation of each pup's personality.

A reputable breeder might tell you which Beagle puppy is appropriate for your home situation and personality. They may not allow you to choose the puppy, although they certainly will take your preference into consideration.

Some breeders, on the other hand, believe it's important for you to be heavily involved in selecting a puppy from the litter. They will let their puppy buyers make the decision on which pup to take home because not everyone is looking for the same things in a dog. Some people want a quiet, laidback attitude. Others want an outgoing, active dog. When

A smart buyer, who carefully screens breeders, will find a healthy and happy Beagle puppy.

Questions to Expect
Be prepared for the breeder to ask you some questions, too.

1. Have you previously owned a Beagle?

The breeder is trying to gauge how familiar you are with the breed. If you have never owned one, illustrate your knowledge of Beagles by telling the breeder about your research.

2. Do you have children? What are their ages?

Some breeders are wary about selling a dog to families with younger children. This isn't a steadfast rule, and some breeders only insist on meeting the children to see how they handle puppies. It all depends on the breeder.

3. How long have you wanted a Beagle?

This helps a breeder know if this purchase is an impulse buy or a carefully thought-out decision. Buying on impulse is one of the biggest mistakes owners can make. Be patient.

Join Club Beagle to get a complete list of questions a breeder should ask you. Click on "Downloads" at: **DogChannel.com/Club-Beagle**

pups are old enough to go to their new homes at roughly 8 to 10 weeks of age, these breeders prefer you make your own decision because no one can tell at this age which pup will make the most intelligent or affectionate dog. The color, sex and markings are obvious, but that is about all you can tell for sure at this age. Everything else being equal — size, health, etc. — some breeders suggest picking the pup whom you have a gut feeling for.

The chemistry between a buyer and puppy is important and should also play a role in

When choosing a puppy, keep an eye out for health-related problems that could be a sign of poor breeding.

With the popularity of Beagles, shelters and rescue groups across the country are often inundated with sweet, loving examples of the breed — from the tiniest puppies to senior dogs,

petite females to strapping males. Often, to get the Beagle of your dreams, it takes a trip to the local shelter. Or, perhaps you could find your ideal dog waiting patiently in the arms of a foster parent at a nearby rescue group. It just takes a bit of effort, patience and a willingness to find the right dog for your family, not just the cutest dog on the block.

The perks of owning a Beagle are plentiful: companionship, unconditional love, true loyalty and laughter, just to name a few. So why choose the adoption option? Because you will be literally saving a life!

Owners of adopted dogs swear they're more grateful and loving than any dog they've owned before. It's almost as if they knew what dire fate awaited them, and are so thankful. Beagles, known for their people-pleasing personalities, seem to embody this mentality wholeheartedly when they're rescued. And they want to give something back. Another perk: Almost all adopted dogs come fully vetted, with proper medical treatment,

vaccinations, as well as being spayed or neutered. Some are even licensed and microchipped.

Don't disregard older dogs, thinking the only good pair-up is between you and a puppy. Adult Beagles are more established behaviorally and personality-wise, helping to better mesh their characteristics with yours in this game of matchmaker. Puppies are always in high demand, so if you open your options to include adults, you will have a better chance of adopting quickly. Plus, adult dogs are often housetrained, more calm, chew-proof, and don't need to be taken outside in the middle of the night ... five times ... in the pouring rain.

The National Beagle Club of America offers rescue support information, or log onto Petfinder. com, which has a searchable database that enables you to find a Beagle in your area who needs a break in the form of a compassionate owner like you. More websites and information can be found in *Resources*, chapter 13, on page 166.

determining which pup goes to which home. When possible, make numerous visits to see the puppies, and in effect, let a puppy choose you. Usually, there will be one puppy who spends more time with a buyer and is more comfortable relaxing and sitting with, or on, a certain person.

CHECKING FOR BEAGLE QUALITIES

Whether you are dealing with a breeder who wants to pick a pup for you or lets you make the decision alone, consider several points when evaluating the pup you may end up calling your own. The puppy should be outgoing, not skittish in any way. He should be forgiving of correction and not too mouthy. The pup should readily follow you, be willing to snuggle in your lap and be turned onto his back without a problem.

Proper temperament is very important. A Beagle puppy who has a dominant personality requires an experienced owner who will be firm during training. A puppy who is a little shy requires heavy socialization to build his confidence.

You also can evaluate a Beagle puppy's temperament on your own. The temperament of the pups can be evaluated by spending some time watching them. If you can visit the pups and observe them first together with their littermates, then you can see how they interact with each other. You may be able to pinpoint which ones are the bullies and which ones are more submissive. In general, look for a puppy who is more interested in you than in his littermates. Then, take each pup individually to a new location away from the rest of the litter. Put the puppy down on the ground, walk away and see how he reacts away from the security of his littermates. The puppy may be afraid at first, but he should gradually recover and start checking out the new surroundings

D-I-Y TEMPERAMENT TEST

Puppies come in a wide assortment of temperaments to suit almost everyone. If you are looking for a dog who is easily trainable and a good companion to your

---

Breeder Q&A
Here are some questions you should ask a breeder and the answers you want to receive.

JOIN OUR ONLINE
Club Beagle™

Q. How often do you have litters available?

A. You want to hear "once or twice a year" or "occasionally" because a breeder who doesn't have litters that often is probably more concerned with the quality of his puppies, rather than with making money.

Q. What kinds of health problems do Beagles have?

A. Beware of a breeder who says, "none." Every breed has health issues. For Beagles, some health problems include Beagle pain syndrome, epiphyseal dysplasia, epilepsy, hypothyroidism and chronic hip dysplasia.

Get a complete list of questions to ask a Beagle breeder — and the correct answers — at Club Beagle. Log onto **DogChannel.com/Club-Beagle** and click on "Downloads."

family, you most likely want a puppy with a medium temperament.

Temperament testing can help you determine the type of disposition your potential puppy possesses. A pup with a medium temperament will have the following reactions to these various tests, best conducted when the pup is 7 weeks old.

Step 1. To test a pup's social attraction and his confidence in approaching humans, coax him toward you by kneeling down and clapping your hands gently. A pup who has a medium temperament comes readily, tail up or down.

Step 2. To test a pup's eagerness to follow you, walk away from him while he is watching you. He should follow you, tail up.

Step 3. To see how well a pup handles restraint, kneel down and roll the pup gently on his back. Using a light but firm touch, hold him in this position with one hand for

30 seconds. The Beagle pup should settle down after some initial struggle at first and offer some or steady eye contact.

Step 4. To evaluate a puppy's level of social dominance, stand up, then crouch

You don't have to wait until your puppy is home to study his personality; you should definitely do a temperament test before you purchase a pup.

Food intolerance is the inability of a dog to completely digest certain foods. Puppies who may have done very well on their mother's milk may not do well on cow's milk. The result of this food intolerance may be loose bowels, passing gas and stomach pains. These are the only obvious symptoms of food intolerance, which makes diagnosis difficult.

down beside the pup and stroke him from head to back. A Beagle puppy with a medium temperament — neither too dominant nor too submissive — should cuddle up to you and lick your face, or squirm and lick your hands.

Step 5. An additional test of a pup's dominance is to bend over, cradle the pup under his belly with your fingers interlaced and palms up, and elevate him just off the ground. Hold him there for 30 seconds. The pup should not struggle and should be relaxed, or he should struggle and then settle down and lick you.

PHYSICAL FEATURES

To assess a puppy's health, take a deliberate, thorough look at each part of his body. Signs of a healthy puppy include bright eyes, a healthy coat, a good appetite and firm stool.

Watch for a telltale link between physical and mental health. A healthy Beagle, as with any breed of puppy, will display a happier, more positive attitude than an unhealthy puppy. A Beagle puppy's belly should not be over extended or hard, as

this may be a sign of worms. If you are around the litter long enough to witness a bowel movement, the stool should be solid, and the pup should not show any signs of discomfort. Look into the pup's eyes, too; they should be bright and full of life.

When purchasing a Beagle puppy, buyers hear from breeders that these dogs are just like any other puppy — times 10! They are very smart, loving and sometimes stubborn, and they often have their own agendas. If a prospective owner isn't willing to spend a fair amount of time with a Beagle, then the breed is not for them. A Beagle wants to be with people and is quite similar to a 7-year-old boy in the sense that he needs attention and consistent reinforcement for behavioral parameters. Once through adolescence, however, a Beagle is the best friend, guardian and companion a person or family could have.

PUPPY PARTICULARS

Here are signs to look for when picking a Beagle puppy from a breeder. When in doubt, ask the breeder which puppy they think has the best personality/temperament to fit your lifestyle.

1. Look at the area where the pups spend most of their time. It's OK if they play outdoors part of the day, but they should sleep indoors at night so the pups can interact with people and become accustomed to hearing ordinary household noises. This builds a solid foundation for a raising well-socialized and secure Beagle puppy. The puppies' area should be clean, well-lit, have fresh drinking water and interesting toys.

2. Sure, you're only buying one puppy, but make sure to see all of the puppies in the litter. By 5 weeks of age, healthy pups will begin playing with one another and should be lively and energetic. It's OK if they're asleep when you visit, but stay long enough to see them wake up. Once they're up, they shouldn't be lethargic or weak, as this may be a sign of illness.

3. Pups should be confident and eager to greet you. A Beagle pup who is shy or fearful and stays in the corner may be sick or insecure. Although some introverted pups come out of their shells later on, many do not. These dogs will always be fearful as adults and are not good choices for an active, noisy family with or without children, or for people who have never had a dog before. They frighten easily and will require a tremendous amount of training and socialization in order to live a happy life.

Choose a pup who is happy and eager to interact with you but reject the one who is too shy or too bossy. These temperament types are a challenge to deal with and require a tremendous amount of training. The perfect Beagle puppy personality is somewhere between the two extremes.

4. If it's feeding time during your visit, all pups should be eager to gobble up their food. A puppy who refuses to eat may signal illness.

5. The dog's skin should be smooth, clean and shiny without any sores or bumps. Puppies should not be biting or scratching at themselves continuously, which could signal fleas.

6. After 10 to 12 days, eyes should be open and clear without any redness or discharges. Pups should not be scratching at their eyes, as this may cause an infection or signal irritation.

7. Vomiting or coughing more than once is not normal. If so, a Beagle pup might be ill and should visit the veterinarian immediately.

8. Visit long enough to observe the Beagle pups eliminate. All stools should be firm without being watery or bloody. These are signs of illness or that a puppy has worms.

9. Beagle puppies should walk or run freely without limping.

10. A healthy Beagle puppy who is getting enough to eat should not be skinny. You should be able to slightly feel his ribs if you rub his abdomen, but you should not be able to see the ribs protruding.

BREEDER PAPERS

Everything today comes with an instruction manual. When you purchase a Beagle puppy, it's no different. A reputable breeder should give you a registration application; a sales contract; a health guarantee; your puppy's complete health records; a three-, four- or five-generation pedigree; and some general information on behavior, care, conformation, health and training.

Registration Application. This document from the AKC or UKC assigns your puppy a number and identifies him by listing his date of birth, the names of his parents and shows that he is registered as a purebred Beagle. It doesn't prove whether or not your dog is a show- or a pet-quality Beagle and doesn't provide any health guarantee.

Sales Contract. A reputable breeder should discuss the terms of the contract with you before asking you to sign it. This is a written understanding of both of your expectations and shows that the breeder cares about the pup's welfare throughout his life. The contract can include such terms as requiring you to keep the dog indoors at night, spaying or neutering if the puppy is not going to be a show dog, providing routine vet care and assurance that you'll feed your dog a healthy diet. Most responsible breeders will ask that you take your dog to obedience classes and earn a Canine Good Citizen title (an AKC training certification for dogs who exhibit good manners) before he is 2 years old. Many breeders also require new owners to have totally secure fencing and gates around their yard. Beagles are incredible escape artists, and they will find a way out of the yard if there's even the slightest opening.

Healthy Puppy Signs

Here are a few things you should look for when selecting a puppy from a litter.

1. **NOSE:** It should be slightly moist to the touch, but there shouldn't be excessive discharge. The puppy should not be sneezing or sniffling persistently.

2. **SKIN AND COAT:** Your Beagle puppy's coat should be soft and shiny, without flakes or excessive shedding. Watch out for patches of missing hair, redness, bumps or sores. The pup should have a pleasant smell. Check for parasites, such as fleas or ticks.

3. **BEHAVIOR:** A healthy Beagle puppy may be sleepy, but he should not be lethargic. A healthy puppy will be playful at times, not isolated in a corner. You should see occasional bursts of energy and interaction with littermates. When it's mealtime, a healthy puppy will take an interest in his food.

There are more signs to look for when picking out the perfect Beagle puppy for your lifestyle. Download the list at **DogChannel.com/Club-Beagle**

A reputable breeder will be eager to provide you with as much information as he can about the Beagle breed.

Health Guarantee. This includes a letter, signed by a veterinarian, stating that your puppy has been thoroughly examined and is healthy. It also states that the breeder will replace your dog if he were to develop any type of genetic, life-threatening illness during his lifetime.

Health Records. Here's everything you want to know about your puppy's and his parents' health. It should include the dates the puppy was vaccinated, dewormed and examined by a veterinarian for signs of heart murmur, plus the parents' test results for the presence or absence of hip and elbow dysplasia, heart problems and luxated patellas.

Pedigree. Breeders should provide you with a copy of the puppy's pedigree. Many breeders also have photos of the dog's ancestors that they will proudly share with you.

Extra Information. The best Beagle breeders pride themselves on providing for their buyers a notebook full of the latest information on Beagle behavior, care, conformation, health and training. Be sure to read it because it will provide invaluable help and guidance while you and your family raise your Beagle.

it's a Fact

The breed is seen frequently in the winner's circle at conformation shows, and some 3,000 sanctioned Beagle Field Trials are held each year. Despite all these competitions, most hunting Beagles hunt individually or in pairs with their masters. The breed's name has even become a verb as enthusiasts out on the hunt or involved in field trials are said to be "beagling."

CHAPTER
4

HOME

ESSENTIALS

Don't for one second think that a Beagle would prefer to live out in the field with hunters! He, like every other breed, wants to live in the best accommodations with plenty of toys, soft bedding and other luxuries. Your home is now his home, too; and, before you even bring that new puppy or rescue dog into his new forever home, be a smart owner and make your home accessible for him.

In fact, in order for him to grow into a stable, well-adjusted dog, he has to feel comfortable in his surroundings. Remember, he is leaving the warmth and security of his mother and littermates, as well as the familiarity of the only place he has ever known, so it is important to make his transition to your home — his new home — as easy as possible.

PUPPY-PROOFING

Aside from making sure that your Beagle will be comfortable in your home, you also have to ensure that your home is safe, which means taking the proper precautions to keep your pup away from things that are dangerous for him.

it's a Fact

Dangers lurk indoors and outdoors. Keep your curious Beagle from investigating your shed and garage. Antifreeze and fertilizers, such as those you would use for roses, can kill any dog. Keep these items on high shelves that are out of reach.

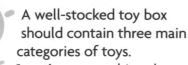

SMART TIP!

A well-stocked toy box should contain three main categories of toys.
1. **action** — anything that you can throw or roll and get things moving
2. **distraction** — durable toys that make dogs work for a treat
3. **comfort** — soft, stuffed "security blankets"

The best Beagle homes have plenty of toys to keep Beagles busy and out of trouble.

Puppy-proof your home inside and out before bringing your Beagle home for the first time. Place breakables out of reach. If he is limited to certain places within the house, keep potentially dangerous items in off-limit areas. If your Beagle is going to spend time in a crate, make sure that there isn't anything near it that he can reach if he sticks his curious little nose or paws through the openings.

The outside of your home must also be safe. Your pup will want to run and explore the yard, and he should be granted that freedom — as long as you are there to supervise. Do not let a fence give you a false sense of security; you would be surprised how crafty and persistent a Beagle puppy can be in figuring out how to dig under a fence or squeeze his way through holes. The remedy is to make the fence well embedded into the ground. Be sure to repair or secure any gaps in the fence. Check the fence periodically to ensure that it is in good shape and make repairs as needed; a very determined puppy may work on the same spot until he is able to get through.

The following are a few common problem areas to watch out for in the home.

■ **Electrical cords and wiring:** No electrical cord or wiring is safe. Many office-supply stores sell products to keep wires gathered under computer desks, as well as products that prevent office chair wheels (and puppy teeth) from damaging electrical cords. If you do have exposed cords and wires, these products aren't very expensive and can be used to keep a puppy out of trouble.

■ **Trash cans:** Don't waste your time trying to train your Beagle not to get into the trash. Simply put the garbage behind a cabinet door and use a child-safe lock, if necessary. Dogs love bathroom trash, which consists of items that can be extremely dangerous (i.e., cotton balls, cotton

Once you find the perfect puppy, your work has just begun. There's plenty of things you need to take care of around the house to ensure your dog's health and safety.

swabs, used razors, dental floss, etc.)! Put the bathroom trash can in a cabinet under the sink and make sure you always shut the door to the bathroom.

■ **Household cleaners:** Make sure your Beagle puppy doesn't have access to any of these deadly chemicals. Keep them behind closed cabinet doors, using child-safe locks, if necessary.

■ **Pest control sprays and poisons:** Chemicals to control ants or other pests should never be used in the house, if possible. Your Beagle pup doesn't have to directly ingest these poisons to become ill; if he steps in the poison, he can experience toxic effects by licking his paws. Roach motels and other toxic pest traps are also yummy to dogs, so don't drop these behind couches or cabinets; if there's room for a roach motel, there's room for a determined Beagle.

■ **Fabric:** Here's one you might not think about: Some puppies have a habit of licking blankets, upholstery, rugs or carpets. Though this habit seems fairly innocuous, over time the fibers from the upholstery or carpet can accumulate in your dog's stomach and cause a blockage. If you see your dog licking these items, remove the item or prevent him from having contact with it.

■ **Prescriptions, painkillers, supplements and vitamins:** Keep all medications in a cabinet. Also, be very careful when taking your prescription medications, supplements or vitamins: How often have you dropped a pill? You can be sure that your

The Beagle's powerful olfactory senses may lead him toward potentially dangerous household items; store these things up high or behind closed doors to prevent injuries.

The first thing you should always do before your puppy comes home is to lie on the ground and look around. You want to be able to see everything your puppy is going to see. For your puppy, the world is one big chew toy.

— Cathleen Stamm, rescue volunteer in San Diego, Calif.

Beagle puppy will be in between your legs and will gobble up the pill before you even start to say "No!" Dispense your pills carefully and without your Beagle present.

■ **Miscellaneous loose items:** If it's not bolted to the floor, your puppy is likely to give the item a taste test. Socks, coins, children's toys, game pieces, cat toys — you name it: If it's on the floor, it's worth a try. Make sure the floors in your home are picked up and free of clutter.

FAMILY INTRODUCTIONS

Everyone in the house will be excited about your puppy's homecoming and will want to pet and play with him, but it's best to make the introduction low-key so as not to overwhelm your puppy. He already will be apprehensive. It is the first time he has been separated from his mother, littermates and breeder, and the ride to your home is likely to be the first time he has been in a car. The last thing you want to do is smother your Beagle pup, as this will only frighten him further. This is not to say that human contact is unnecessary at this stage because this is the time when a connection between the pup and his human family is formed. Gentle petting and soothing words should help console your Beagle, as well as putting him down and letting him explore on his own (under your watchful eye, of course).

Your pup may approach family members or may busy himself exploring for a while. Gradually, each person should spend some time with the pup, one at a time, crouching down to get as close to the Beagle's level as possible, letting him sniff their hands before petting him gently. He definitely needs human attention, and he needs to be touched; this is how to form an immediate bond. Just remember that the pup is experiencing a lot of things for the first

time, all at once. There are new people, new noises, new smells and new things to investigate. Be gentle, be affectionate and be as comforting as you can possibly be.

PUP'S FIRST NIGHT HOME

You have traveled home with your new puppy safely in his crate. He may have already been to the vet for a thorough check-up — he's been weighed, his papers

For a peaceful night's sleep, ask the breeder to give you something from your puppy's old bed that will comfort him in his new doggy digs.

examined, perhaps he's even been vaccinated and dewormed as well. Your Beagle has met and licked the whole family, including the excited children and the less-than-happy cat. He's explored his area, his new bed, the yard and everywhere else he's permitted. He's eaten his first meal at home and relieved himself in the proper place. Your Beagle has heard lots of new sounds,

SMART TIP!

When you are unable to watch your Beagle puppy, put her in a crate or an exercise pen on an easily cleanable floor. If she has an accident on carpeting, clean it completely and meticulously, so that it doesn't smell like her potty forever.

smelled new friends and seen more of the outside world than ever before. This was just the first day! He's worn out and is ready for bed — or so you think!

Remember, this is your puppy's first night sleeping alone. His mother and littermates are no longer at paw's length, and he's scared, cold and lonely. Be reassuring to your new family member. This is not the time to spoil your Beagle, however, and give in to his inevitable whining. Puppies whine. They whine to let others know where they are and hopefully to get company out of it. Place your Beagle puppy in his new bed or crate in his room and close the door. He may be merciful and fall asleep without a peep. If the inevitable occurs, ignore the whining; he is fine. Do not give in and visit your Beagle puppy. He will fall asleep eventually.

Many breeders recommend placing a piece of bedding from his former home in his new bed so that he will recognize the scent of his littermates. Others still advise placing a hot water bottle in his bed for warmth. The latter may be a good idea provided the pup doesn't attempt to suckle.

Your Beagle's first night can be somewhat terrifying for him. Remember that *you* set the tone of nighttime at your house. Unless you want to play with your pup every night at 10 p.m., midnight and 2 a.m., don't initiate the habit; let your puppy sleep. Your family will thank you!

SMART TIP!

9-1-1! If you don't know whether the plant, food or "stuff" your Beagle just ate is toxic to dogs, call the ASPCA's Animal Poison Control Center (888-426-4435). Be prepared to provide your puppy's age and weight, her symptoms — if any — and how much of the plant, chemical or substance she ingested, as well as how long ago you think she came into contact with the substance. The ASPCA charges a consultation fee for this service.

PET-SUPPLY STORE SHOPPING

It's fun shopping for new things for a new puppy. From training to feeding and sleeping to playing, your new Beagle will need a few items to make life comfy, easy and fun. Be prepared with a list of items, and visit your local pet-supply store before you bring home your new family member.

◆ **Collar and ID tag:** Accustom your dog to wearing a collar the first day you bring him home. Not only will a collar and ID tag help your puppy in the event that he becomes lost, but collars are also an important training tool. If your Beagle gets into trouble, the collar will act as a handle, helping you divert him to a more appropriate behavior. Make sure the collar fits snugly enough so your Beagle cannot wriggle out of it, but is loose enough so that it will not be uncomfortably tight around

---

NOTABLE & QUOTABLE

Playing with toys from puppyhood encourages good behavior and social skills throughout your dog's life. A happy, playful dog is a content and well-adjusted one. Also, because all puppies chew to soothe their gums and help loosen puppy teeth, dogs should always have easy access to several different toys.

— *dog trainer and author Harrison Forbes of Savannah, Tenn.*

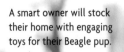

A smart owner will stock their home with engaging toys for their Beagle pup.

Keep a crate in your vehicle and take your Beagle along when you visit the drive-thru at the bank or your favorite fast-food restaurant. She can watch interactions, hear interesting sounds and maybe earn a treat.

his neck. You should be able to fit a finger between your pup's neck and the collar. Collars come in many styles, but for starting out, a simple buckle collar with an easy-release snap works great.

◆ **Leash:** For training or just for taking a stroll down the street, a leash is your Beagle's vehicle to explore the outside world. Like collars, leashes come in a variety of styles and materials. A 6-foot nylon leash is a popular choice because it is lightweight and durable. As your pup grows and gets used to walking on the leash, you may want to purchase a flexible leash. These leashes allow you to extend the length to give your dog a broader area to explore or to shorten the length to keep your dog closer to you.

◆ **Bowls:** Your Beagle will need two bowls: one for his water and one for his food. You may want two sets of bowls, one for inside and one for outside, depending on where your dog will be fed and where he will be spending time. Bowls should be sturdy enough so that they don't tip over easily. (Most have reinforced bottoms that prevent tipping.) Bowls usually are made of metal, ceramic or plastic, and should be easy to clean.

◆ **Crate:** A multipurpose crate serves as a bed, housetraining tool and travel carrier. It also is the

ideal doggie den — a bedroom of sorts — that your Beagle can retire to when he wants to rest or just needs a break. The crate should be large enough for your dog to stand, turn around and lie down. You don't want any more room than this — especially if you're planning on using the crate to housetrain your Beagle — because he will eliminate in one corner and lie down in another. Get a crate that is big enough for your dog when he is an adult; then, use dividers to limit the space when he's a puppy.

◆ **Bed:** A plush dog bed will make sleeping and resting more comfortable for your Beagle. Dog beds come in all shapes, sizes and colors, but your dog just needs one that is soft and large enough for him to stretch out on. Because puppies and rescue dogs may not always be housetrained, it's helpful to buy a bed that can be easily washed. If your Beagle will be sleeping

Your Beagle deserves some luxury items, too! Find appropriate pet furniture at your local pet-supply store, or pick up some used furniture at a thrift store that your pup can call his own.

in a crate, a nice crate pad and a small blanket that he can burrow in will help him feel more at home. Replace the blanket if it becomes ragged and starts to fall apart because your Beagle's nails could get caught in it.

◆ **Gate:** Similar to those used for toddlers, gates help keep your Beagle confined to one room or area when you can't supervise him. Gates also work to keep your dog out of areas you don't want him in. Gates are available in many styles. Make sure you choose one with openings small enough so your puppy can't squeeze through the bars or any gaps.

◆ **Toys:** Keep your dog occupied and entertained by providing him with an array

of fun toys. Teething puppies like to chew — in fact, chewing is a physical need for pups as they are teething — and everything from your shoes to the leather couch to the fancy

Make special areas of your house hound-friendly, places he can call his own. These areas should be, however, located near where the family spends most of its time.

rug are fair game. Divert your Beagle's chewing instincts with durable toys like bones made of nylon or hard rubber.

Other fun toys include rope toys, treat-dispensing toys and balls. Make sure the toys and bones don't have small parts that could break off and be swallowed, causing your dog to choke. Stuffed toys can become destuffed, and an overly excited puppy may ingest the stuffing or the squeaker. Check your Beagle's toys regularly and replace them if they become frayed or show signs of wear.

◆ **Cleaning supplies:** Until your Beagle puppy is housetrained, you will be doing a lot of cleaning. Accidents will occur, which is acceptable in the beginning because your puppy doesn't know any better. All you can do is be prepared to clean up any accidents. Old rags, towels, newspapers and a stain-and-odor remover are good to have on hand.

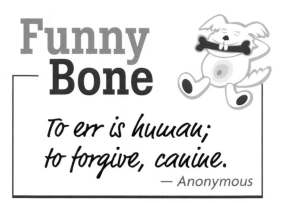

Funny Bone

*To err is human;
to forgive, canine.*

— *Anonymous*

BEYOND THE BASICS

The basic items discussed previously are the bare necessities. You will find out what else you and your new dog need as you go along — grooming supplies, flea/tick protection — and these things will vary depending on your situation. It is important, however, that you have everything you need to make your Beagle comfortable in his new home.

Some ordinary household items make great toys for your Beagle — as long you make sure they are safe. Tennis balls, plastic water bottles, old towels and more can be transformed into fun with a little creativity. You can find a list of homemade toys at **DogChannel.com/Club-Beagle**

HOUSETRAINING

Unexciting as it may be, the house-training part of puppy rearing greatly affects the budding relationship between a smart owner and his puppy — particularly when it becomes a source of ongoing contention. Fortunately, armed with suitable knowledge, patience and common sense, you'll find housetraining progresses at a relatively smooth rate. That leaves more time for the important things, like cuddling your adorable puppy, showing him off and laughing at his high jinks.

The answer to successful housetraining is total supervision and management — crates, tethers, exercise pens and leashes — until you know your dog has developed preferences for outside surfaces (grass, gravel, concrete) instead of carpet, tile or hardwood. Then, he'll understand that potty happens only outside.

IN THE BEGINNING

For the first two to three weeks of a puppy's life, his mother helps him eliminate. The mother also keeps the whelping box or "nest area" clean. When pups begin to walk around and eat on their own, they choose where they eliminate. You can train your

it's a Fact — **Ongoing housetraining difficulties may indicate your pup has a health problem,** warranting a vet check. A urinary infection, parasites, a virus, and other nasty issues can greatly affect your puppy's ability to hold pee or poop.

puppy to relieve himself wherever you choose, but this must be somewhere suitable. You should bear in mind from the outset that when your puppy is old enough to go out in public places, you must be considerate and pick up after him. You will always have to carry with you a small plastic bag or poop scoop.

Outdoor training includes such surfaces as grass, soil and concrete. Indoor training usually means training your dog on newspaper. When deciding on the surface and location that you will want your Beagle to use, be sure it is going to be permanent. Training your dog on grass and then changing two months later is extremely difficult for the dog as well as the owner.

Next, choose the cue you will use each and every time you want your puppy to eliminate. "Let's go," "hurry up" and "potty" are examples of cues commonly used by smart dog owners.

Get in the habit of giving your puppy the chosen relief cue before you take him out. That way, when he becomes an adult, you will be able to determine if he wants to go out when you ask him. A confirmation will be signs of interest, such as wagging his tail, watching you intently or going to the door.

LET'S START WITH THE CRATE

Dogs are clean animals by nature and dislike soiling where they sleep and eat. This fact makes a crate a useful tool for housetraining. When purchasing a new crate, consider that an appropriately sized crate will allow adequate room for an adult Beagle to stand full-height, lie on his side without scrunching and to turn around easily. If debating plastic versus wire crates, short-haired breeds sometimes prefer the warmer, draft-blocking quality of plastic, while furry dogs often like the cooling airflow of a wire crate.

Some crates come with a movable wall that reduces the interior size to provide enough space for your puppy to stand, turn and lie down, while not allowing him room to soil one end and sleep in the other. The problem is that if your puppy potties in the crate anyway, the divider forces him to lie in his own excrement.

This can work against you by desensitizing your puppy against his normal, instinctive revulsion to resting where he has just eliminated. If scheduling permits you or a responsible family member to clean the crate soon after it's soiled, then you can continue to cratetrain because limiting crate size does encourage your puppy to hold it. Otherwise, give him enough room to move away from an unclean area until he's better able to control his elimination.

Needless to say, not every puppy adheres to this guideline. If your Beagle moves along at a faster pace, thank your lucky stars. Should he progress slower, accept it and remind yourself that he'll improve. Be aware that puppies frequently hold it longer at night than during the day. Just because your puppy sleeps for six or more hours through the night, it does not mean he can hold it that long during the more active daytime hours.

One last bit of advice on the crate: Place it in the corner of a high-traffic room, such as the family room or kitchen. Social and curious by nature, dogs like to feel included in

Be aware of your puppy's signals that he has to potty, such as sniffing the ground, spinning around or intently staring at you.

Set up a potty schedule to facilitate housetraining. Include taking your pup out to potty after a meal and a nap.

family happenings. Creating a quiet retreat by putting the crate in an unused area may seem like a good idea, but results in your puppy feeling insecure and isolated. Watching his people pop in and out of the crate room reassures your puppy that he's not forgotten.

A PUP'S GOT NEEDS

Your puppy needs to relieve himself after play periods, after each meal, after he has been sleeping and any time he indicates that he is looking for a place to urinate or defecate.

The urinary and intestinal tract muscles of young puppies are not fully developed. Therefore, like human babies, puppies need to relieve themselves frequently. Take your puppy out often — every hour for an 8-week-old, for example — and always immediately after sleeping and eating. The older your puppy, the less often he will need to relieve himself. Finally, as a mature, healthy adult, he will require only three to five relief trips per day.

HOUSING HELPS

Because the types of housing and control you provide for your Beagle puppy have a direct relationship on the success of housetraining, you must consider the various aspects of both before beginning training.

The best method to housetraining your puppy is to always use positive reinforcement, as opposed to scolding your puppy for his potty mistakes.

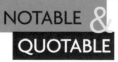

Reward your pup with a high-value treat immediately after he potties to reinforce going in the proper location, then play for a short time afterward. This teaches that good things happen after pottying outside! — Victoria Schade, certified pet dog trainer, from Annandale, Va.

SMART TIP!

If you acquire your Beagle puppy at 8 weeks of age, expect to take her out at least six to eight times a day. By the time she's about 6 months old, potty trips will be down to three to five times a day. A rule of thumb is to take your puppy out in hourly intervals that are equal to her age in months.

Taking a new puppy home and turning him loose in your house can be compared to turning a child loose in a sports arena, and telling the child the place is all his! The sheer enormity of the place would be too much for him to handle. Instead, offer your puppy clearly defined areas where he can play, sleep, eat and live. A room where the family gathers is the obvious choice.

Puppies are social animals and need to feel like they are a part of the pack right from the start. Hearing your voice, watching you while you are doing things and smelling you nearby are all positive reinforcers that he is now a member of your pack. Usually a family room, the kitchen or a nearby adjoining breakfast area is ideal for providing safety and security for puppy and owner.

Within that room, there should be a smaller area that your Beagle puppy can call his own. An alcove, a wire or fiberglass dog crate, or a fenced (not boarded!) corner from which he can view the activities of his new family will be fine. The designated area should contain clean bedding and a toy. Water must always be available, in a nonspill container, once your dog is housetrained.

IN CONTROL

By control, we mean helping your puppy to create a lifestyle pattern that will be compatible to that of his human pack (you!). Just as we guide children to learn our way of life, we must show our Beagle pup when it is time to play, eat, sleep, exercise and entertain himself.

Having housetraining problems with your Beagle? Ask other Beagle owners for advice and tips, or post your own success story to encourage other owners. Log onto **DogChannel.com/ Club-Beagle** and click on "Community."

SMART TIP!

When proximity prevents you from going home at lunch or during periods when overtime crops up, make alternative arrangements for getting your puppy out. Hire a pet-sitting or walking service, or enlist the aid of an obliging neighbor willing to help.

Your puppy should always sleep in his crate. He should also learn that, during times of household confusion and a stir of human activity, such as at breakfast when family members are preparing for the day, he can play by himself in relative safety and comfort in his designated area. Each time you leave your Beagle alone, he should understand exactly where he is supposed to stay.

Puppies are chewers. They cannot tell the difference between lamp cords, television wires, shoes or table legs. Chewing into a television wire, for example, can be fatal to your puppy, while a shorted wire can start a fire in the house.

If your puppy chews on the arm of the chair when he is alone, you probably will discipline him angrily when you get home. Thus, he makes the association that your coming home means he is going to be punished. (He will not remember chewing the chair and is incapable of making the association of the discipline with his naughty deed.)

Other times of excitement, such as during family parties, can be fun for your puppy, provided that he can view the activities from the security of his designated area. He is not underfoot, and he is not being fed all sorts of tidbits that will probably cause him stomach distress, yet he still feels a part of the fun.

SCHEDULE A SOLUTION

A puppy should be taken to his relief area each time he is released from his designated area, after meals, after play sessions and when he first awakens in the morning (at 8 weeks of age, this can mean 5 a.m.!). Your puppy will indicate that he's ready "to go" by circling or sniffing busily; do not misinterpret these signs. For a puppy less than 10 weeks of age, a routine of taking him out every hour is necessary. As your puppy grows, he will be able to wait for longer periods of time.

Keep potty trips to your puppy's relief area short. Stay in the area for no more than 5 or 6 minutes, and then return inside the house. If your puppy potties during that time, lavishly praise him and then immediately take him indoors. If he does not potty, but he has an accident later when you go back indoors, pick him up, say "No!" and return to his relief area. Wait a few minutes, then return to the house again. Never hit your Beagle puppy or rub his face in urine or excrement when he has had an accident.

Once indoors, put your Beagle puppy in his crate until you have had time to clean up his accident. Then release him to the family area and watch him more closely than before. Chances are, his accident was a result of your not picking up his potty signals or waiting too long before offering him the opportunity to relieve himself. Never hold a grudge against your puppy for accidents.

Let your Beagle puppy learn that going outdoors means it is time to relieve himself, and not a time to play. Once your puppy is trained, he will be able to play indoors and outdoors and still differentiate between the times for play versus the times to take a potty break.

Nothing is better than a Beagle who knows potty breaks are held outdoors, not indoors!

Help your puppy develop regular hours for naps, being alone, playing by himself and just resting — all in his crate. Encourage him to entertain himself while you are busy elsewhere. Let him learn that having you nearby is comforting, but it's not your main purpose in life to provide him with undivided attention at all hours of the day.

Each time you put your Beagle puppy in his own area, use the same cue, whatever suits you best. Soon your Beagle pup will eagerly run to his crate or designtated area when he hears you say those words.

Remember that one of the primary ingredients in housetraining your puppy is control. Regardless of your lifestyle, there will always be occasions when you will need to have a place where your dog can stay and be happy and safe. Cratetraining is the answer for now and in the future.

A few key elements to always keep in mind are really all you need for a successful housetraining method: consistency, frequency, praise, control and supervision. By following these procedures with a normal, healthy puppy, you and your Beagle will soon be past the stage of accidents and be ready to move on to a full and rewarding life together.

Housetraining a rescue dog may take longer. Be consistent and patient.

10 HOUSETRAINING HOW-TOs

1. Decide where you want your Beagle to eliminate. Take her there every time until she gets the idea. Pick a spot that's easy to access. Remember, puppies have very little time between "gotta go" and "oops."

2. Teach an elimination cue, such as "go potty" or "get busy." Say this every time you take your Beagle to eliminate. Don't keep chanting the cue, just say it once or twice, then keep quiet so you won't distract your hound dog.

3. Calmly praise your dog when she eliminates, but stand there a little longer in case there's more.

4. Keep potty outings for potty only. Take your dog to the designated spot, tell her "go potty" and just stand there. If she needs to eliminate, she will do so within five minutes.

5. Don't punish for potty accidents; punishment can hinder progress. If you catch your Beagle in the act indoors, verbally interrupt but don't scold. Gently carry or lead your pup to the approved spot, let her finish, then praise her.

6. If it's too late to interrupt an accident, scoop the poop or blot up the urine afterward with a paper towel. Immediately take your dog and her deposit (gently!) to the potty area. Place the poop or trace of urine on the ground and praise the pup. If she sniffs at her waste, praise more. Let your Beagle know you're pleased when her waste is in the proper area.

7. Keep track of when and where your Beagle eliminates; this will help you anticipate potty times. Regular meals mean regular elimination, so feed your dog scheduled, measured meals instead of free-feeding (leaving food available at all times).

8. Hang a bell on a sturdy cord from the doorknob. Before you open the door to take your puppy out for potty, shake the string and ring the bell. Most dogs soon realize the connection between the bell ringing and the door opening, then they'll try it out for themselves.

9. Dogs naturally return to re-soil where they've previously eliminated, so thoroughly clean up all accidents. Household cleaners usually will do the job, but special enzyme solutions may work better.

10. If the ground is littered with too much waste, your Beagle may seek a cleaner place to eliminate. Scoop the potty area daily, leaving behind just one "reminder."

VET VISITS AND

EVERYDAY CARE

Your selection of a veterinarian for your Beagle should be based on personal recommendations of the doctor's skills with dogs, and, if possible, hounds and Beagles in particular. If the veterinarian is based nearby, it will be helpful and more convenient because you might have an emergency or need to make multiple visits for treatments.

FIRST STEP: SELECT THE RIGHT VET

All licensed veterinarians should be capable of dealing with routine medical issues such as infections and injuries, as well as the promotion of good health (e.g. vaccinations). If the problem affecting your Beagle is more complex, your vet will refer you to someone with more detailed knowledge of what is wrong. This usually will be a specialist such as a veterinary dermatologist or veterinary ophthalmologist.

Veterinary procedures are very costly, and, as treatments improve, they are going to become more expensive. It is quite acceptable to discuss matters of cost with your vet; if there is more than one treatment option, cost may be a factor in deciding which route to take.

Smart owners will look for a veterinarian before they actually need one. For newbie pet owners, start looking for a veterinarian a month or two before you bring home your new Beagle puppy. That will give you time to meet candidate veterinarians, check out the condition of the clinic, meet the staff and see whom you feel most comfortable with. If you already have a Beagle puppy, look sooner rather than later, preferably not in the midst of a veterinary health crisis.

Second, list the qualities that are important to you. Here are some points to consider or investigate:

Convenience: Proximity to your home, extended hours and drop-off services are helpful for people who work regular business hours, have a busy schedule or don't want to drive far. If you have mobility issues, finding a vet who makes house calls or a service that provides pet transport might be particularly important.

Size: A practice with only one person will ensure that you will always be dealing with the same veterinarian during each and every visit. "That person can really get to know you and your dog," says Bernadine Cruz, D.V.M., of Laguna Hills Animal Hospital in Laguna Hills, Calif. The downside, though, is that the sole practitioner does not have the immediate input of another vet, and if your vet becomes ill or takes time off, you will be out of luck.

A multiple-doctor practice offers consistency if your dog needs to come in unexpectedly on a day when your veterinarian isn't there. Additionally, your vet can quickly consult with his colleagues within the clinic if he's unsure about a diagnosis or a treatment.

If you find a veterinarian within that practice whom you really like, you can make your appointments with that individual, establishing the same kind of bond that you would with a solo practitioner.

Appointment Policies: Some practices are by-appointment only, which could minimize your wait time. However, if a sudden problem arises with your Beagle and all the veterinarians are booked up, they might not be able to squeeze your pet in that day. Some clinics are drop-in only, which is great for impromptu or crisis visits, but without scheduling may involve longer waits to see the next available veterinarian. Some practices offer the best of both worlds by maintaining an appointment schedule but also keeping slots open throughout the day for walk-ins.

Basic vs. Full Service vs. State-of-the-Art: A veterinarian practice with high-tech equipment offers greater diagnostic capabilities and treatment options, important for tricky or difficult cases. However, the cost of pricey equipment is passed along to the client, so you could pay more for routine procedures — the bulk of most pets' appointments. Some practices offer boarding, grooming, training classes and other services on the premises — conveniences some pet owners appreciate.

Fees and Payment Polices: How much is a routine visit? If there is a significant price difference, ask why. If you intend to carry health insurance on your Beagle or want to pay by credit card, check that the clinic accepts those payment options.

FIRST VET VISIT

It is much easier, less costly and more effective to practice preventive medicine than to fight bouts of illness and disease. Properly bred puppies of all breeds come from parents who were selected based upon their genetic disease profile. The puppies' mother should have been vaccinated, free of all internal and external parasites and properly nourished. For these

Face it. Nobody, or no dog, likes to visit the doc. Take your Beagle puppy to visit the office before he actually needs to so he'll learn that it isn't such a bad place.

reasons, a visit to the veterinarian who cared for the mother is recommended if at all possible. The dam passes disease resistance to her puppies, which should last from 8 to 10 weeks. Unfortunately, she can also pass on parasites and infection. This is why knowing about her health is useful in learning more about the health of her puppies.

Now that you have your Beagle puppy home safe and sound, it's time to arrange your pup's first trip to the veterinarian. Perhaps the breeder can recommend someone in the area who specializes in Beagles, or maybe you know other Beagle owners who can suggest a good vet. Either way, you should make an appointment within a couple of days of bringing home your puppy. If possible, see if you can stop for this first vet appointment before going home.

The pup's first vet visit will consist of an overall examination to make sure that your pup does not have any problems that are not apparent to you. The veterinarian also will set up a schedule for the pup's vaccinations; the breeder should inform you of which ones your puppy has already received, and the vet can continue from there.

Your puppy also will have his teeth examined and have his skeletal conformation and general health checked prior to certification by the veterinarian. Puppies in certain breeds have problems with their kneecaps, cataracts and other eye problems, heart murmurs and undescended testicles. They may also have behavioral problems, which your veterinarian can evaluate if he or she has had relevant training.

VACCINATION SCHEDULING

Most vaccinations are given by injection and should only be given by a veterinarian. Both you and the vet should keep a record of the date of the injection, the identification of the vaccine and the amount given. Some veterinarians give a first vaccination at 8 weeks of age, but most dog breeders prefer the course of vaccinations not to commence until about 10 weeks because of their interaction with the antibodies produced by the mother. The vaccination scheduling is usually based on a 15-day cycle. You absolutely must take your vet's advice as to when to vaccinate, as this may differ according to the vaccine used.

Set up a vet visit before you even bring your new dog home, so you can interview the veterinary staff.

Check with your vet about booster immunizations for your growing Beagle puppy.

[Beagle pain syndrome]-affected dogs show signs of severe neck pain and frequently cry out when approached because of fear of being touched. Most adopt a stance with their head held low and their back arched, and they won't bend their necks. They can usually walk, although they place their feet carefully and look as if they are walking on eggshells.

— Natasha Olby, Vet. M.B. and associate professor of neurology at the College of Veterinary Medicine at North Carolina State University

The usual vaccines contain immunizing doses of several different viruses such as distemper, parvovirus, parainfluenza and hepatitis. There are other vaccines available when your puppy is at a greater risk for viral exposures. You should rely on your vet's advice. This is especially true for the booster immunizations. Most vaccination programs require a booster when a puppy is a year old and once a year thereafter. In some cases, circumstances may require more frequent immunizations.

Kennel cough, more formally known as *tracheobronchitis*, is combatted with a vaccine that is sprayed into the dog's nostrils. Kennel cough is usually included in routine vaccinations, but it is often not as effective as the vaccines for other major diseases.

Your veterinarian probably will recommend that your Beagle puppy be fully vaccinated before you take him on outings. There are airborne diseases, parasite eggs in the grass and unexpected visits from other dogs who might be dangerous to your puppy's health. Other dogs are the most harmful reservoir of pathogenic organisms, as everything they may have can be transmitted to your puppy.

6 Months to 1 Year of Age: Unless you intend to breed or show your dog, neutering or spaying your Beagle at 6 months of age is recommended. Discuss this with your veterinarian. Neutering and spaying have proven to be beneficial to male and female puppies, respectively. Besides eliminating the possibility of pregnancy, it inhibits (but does not prevent) breast cancer in females and prostate cancer in male dogs.

Your veterinarian should provide your puppy with a thorough dental evaluation at 6 months of age, ascertaining whether all his permanent teeth have erupted properly. A home dental care regimen should also be initiated at 6 months, including weekly brushing and providing good dental devices (such as nylon bones). Regular

NOTABLE & QUOTABLE

The onset of idiopathic epilepsy generally occurs between the ages of 1 and 5 years. Typical seizures are called tonic-clonic (also known as grand mal) seizures. Your dog may stiffen and fall over with his legs extended, neck arched and head thrown back. He may vocalize, lose control of his bowel and urinary functions, and drool excessively; this is the tonic phase and could last up to 30 seconds.

— Steven Zinderman, D.V.M., medical director at Roadside
Veterinary Clinic in Highland, Mich.

dental care promotes healthy teeth, fresh breath and a longer life.

Dogs Older Than 1 Year: Continue to visit the veterinarian at least once a year as your Beagle's bodily functions begin to change with age. The eyes and ears are no longer as efficient. Liver, kidney and intestinal functions often decline. Proper dietary changes recommended by your veterinarian can make life more pleasant for your aging Beagle and you.

EVERYDAY HAPPENINGS

Keeping your Beagle healthy is a matter of keen observation and quick action when necessary. Knowing what's normal for your dog will help you recognize signs of trouble before they blossom into a full-blown emergency situation.

Even if the problem is minor, such as a cut or scrape, you'll want to care for it immediately to prevent infection, as well as to ensure that your dog doesn't make it worse by chewing or scratching at it. Here's what to do for common, minor injuries or illnesses, and how to recognize and deal with emergencies:

Cuts and Scrapes: For a cut or scrape that's half an inch or smaller, clean the wound with saline solution or warm water and use tweezers to remove any splinters or other debris. Apply an antibiotic oint-

Stay on top of your dog's health by keeping a record of his vaccinations.

Just like with infants, puppies need a series of vaccinations to ensure that they stay healthy during their first year of life. Download a vaccination chart from **DogChannel.com/Club-Beagle** that you can fill out for your Beagle.

ment. No bandage is necessary unless the wound is on a paw, which can pick up dirt when your dog walks on it. Deep cuts with lots of bleeding or those caused by glass or some other object should be treated by your veterinarian.

Cold Symptoms: Dogs don't actually get colds, but they can get illnesses that have similar symptoms, such as coughing, a runny nose or sneezing. Dogs cough for any number of reasons, from respiratory infections to inhaled irritants to congestive heart failure. Take your Beagle to the veterinarian for prolonged coughing, or coughing accompanied by labored breathing, runny eyes and nose, or bloody phlegm.

A runny nose that continues for more than several hours requires veterinary attention, as well. If your Beagle sneezes, he may have some mild nasal irritation that will resolve on its own, but frequent sneezing, especially if it's accompanied by a runny nose, may indicate anything from allergies to an infection or something stuck in his nose.

Vomiting and Diarrhea: Sometimes dogs can suffer minor gastric upset when they consume a new type of food; eat too much too quickly; eat the contents of the trash can; or become excited or anxious. Give your Beagle's stomach a rest by withholding food for 12 hours, and then feeding him a bland diet such as baby food or rice and chicken, gradually returning your dog to his normal food. Vomiting, projectile vomiting or diarrhea that continues for more than 48 hours is another matter. If this happens, immediately take your Beagle to the veterinarian.

MORE HEALTH HINTS

A Beagle's anal glands can cause problems if not periodically evacuated. In the wild, dogs regularly clear their anal glands to mark their territory, but in domestic dogs, this function is no longer necessary. Thus, their contents can build up and clog, causing discomfort. Signs that the anal glands — located on both sides of the anus — need emptying are if a Beagle drags his rear end along the ground or keeps turning around to lick the area of discomfort.

While care must be taken not to cause injury, anal glands can be evacuated by pressing gently on either side of the anal opening and by using a piece of cotton or a tissue to collect the foul-smelling matter. If anal glands are allowed to become impacted, abscesses can form, causing pain and the need for veterinary attention.

Beagles can get into all sorts of mischief, so it is not uncommon for them to swallow something poisonous in the course of their investigations. Obviously, an urgent visit to the vet is required under such circumstances, but if possible, when you call your vet, inform him which poisonous substance has been ingested, because different treatments are needed. Should it be necessary to cause your dog to vomit (which is not always the case with poisoning), a small lump of baking soda, given orally, will have an immediate effect. Alternatively, a small teaspoon of salt or mustard, dissolved in water, will have a similar effect but may be more difficult to administer and take longer to work.

Beagle puppies often have painful fits while they are teething. These are not usually serious and are brief. Of course, you must be certain that the cause is nothing more than teething. Giving a puppy something hard to chew on usually will solve this temporary problem.

Prevention is the best medicine. Keep your Beagle active and you can avoid many health complications.

No matter how careful you are with your precious Beagle, sometimes unexpected injuries happen. Be prepared for an emergency by assembling a canine first-aid kit. Find out what essentials you need on **DogChannel.com/Club-Beagle** — just click on "Downloads."

ON THE TOPIC

When it comes to choosing a breed that's energetic, outgoing, good-tempered and independent, it's difficult to choose a breed better than a Beagle. Beagles love companionship, which may be why Charles Schulz's Snoopy is so often engaged in quaffing down root beer with his *Peanut* friends. Healthwise, Beagles are easy-keepers: Their coat is easy to groom, they generally live more than 12 years and they are not afflicted by a great number of health problems that can't be simply addressed.

But Beagles, like any breed, are still susceptible to certain genetic diseases. For the Beagle breed, those hereditary diseases include Beagle pain syndrome, epiphyseal dysplasia, epilepsy, hypothyroidism, cherry eye and chronic hip dysplasia.

BEAGLE PAIN SYNDROME

Beagle pain syndrome, formally known as steroid responsive meningitis arteritis, is an abnormal immune response that occurs in certain blood vessels enveloping the brain and spinal cord, and sometimes the coronary arteries, resulting in severe meningitis. SRMA is fairly rare, although the National Beagle Club reports it's on the rise. Besides Beagles, it affects Bernese Mountain Dogs, Boxers and German Shorthaired Pointers.

The onset of SRMA typically occurs when a puppy is between 4 and 10 months of age, although it can occur as early as 3 months, and occasionally in much older dogs. The cause of Beagle pain syndrome is unknown. It's likely that genetic factors play a role, because

Beagles as a breed are predisposed to the disease. The search for a diagnosis usually begins at the local veterinarian's office, where X-rays can rule out vertebrae problems. Treatment consists of oral corticosteroids, usually prednisone, although some people use dexamethasone (another class of steroids). If left untreated, the signs tend to wax and wane, but a complete, spontaneous recovery is rare.

EPIPHYSEAL DYSPLASIA

Epiphyseal dysplasia, is a genetic disease in which some of the epiphyseal growth plates of the long bones and vertebral bodies have tiny areas of abnormalities where calcification shows up as stippling or mottling on radiographs. As a result, these bones fail to grow properly within the cartilage precursors and bones, resulting in stunted, twisted limbs; shortened, deformed vertebrae; dwarfism; and joint pain.

This disease shows up early, at about 3 to 4 weeks of age. "The puppy is slow to thrive," explains Beagle breeder Judith Musladin, M.D., formerly with the National Beagle Club's Health and Genetics Committee. "A Beagle is either slow to get up on his legs or, when he does get up on his legs, by 4 weeks of age he isn't comfortable on his legs. The puppy begins to sag and moves with great difficulty."

By 5 or 6 months of age, the disease stabilizes as the growth plates mature. The puppy seems to become more comfortable, although he may walk with a limp and will usually have deformed front or rear legs, a curved back or a shortened neck.

According to a study by researchers at the University of California, Berkeley, the disease is difficult to diagnose in Beagles, in part because of the narrow window of time (3 weeks to 4 months old) for a solid radiographic diagnosis. Diagnosis is made by radiographs, optimally when the pup is about 2 months old and abnormalities in the growth centers can still be observed. By 4 to 6 months old, the growth centers are incorporated into the bone and the telltale abnormalities specific to ED have disappeared.

"If you take an X-ray of the dog with epiphyseal dysplasia at 1 year of age, you'll see arthritic joints but no evidence of the original disease process," Musladin says.

At this time, there is no cure for ED. "It does not affect longevity but affects the dog's comfort," Musladin says. "The dog ends up with a joint that is prone to arthritis. The arthritis becomes more severe as the Beagle ages, but medications can be helpful."

EPILEPSY

Idiopathic epilepsy is a disorder associated with recurrent seizures that are not a consequence of other disorders, such as head trauma, low blood sugar, poisoning, heart disease, kidney or liver failure, or electrolyte imbalances. Seen in dozens of dog breeds, idiopathic epilepsy is one of the most common diseases of the nervous system in dogs. However, it's difficult to diagnose because seizures can occur for several reasons, and there is no actual epilepsy test. Hence, the diagnosis is actually made by eliminating other possible causes — a diagnosis of exclusion.

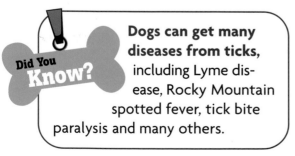

Did You Know? Dogs can get many diseases from ticks, including Lyme disease, Rocky Mountain spotted fever, tick bite paralysis and many others.

"The onset of idiopathic epilepsy generally occurs between the ages of 1 and 5 years," says Steven Zinderman, D.V.M., medical director at Roadside Veterinary Clinic in Highland, Mich. Typical seizures, called tonic-clonic grand mal seizures cause the dog to stiffen, vocalize, lose control of his bowel and urinary function or drool excessively. This tonic phase could last up to 30 seconds.

"The clonic phase follows, during which your dog may paddle his legs as if he were running, experience facial and muscle twitching and chomp his jaws; this could last another 60 seconds," Zinderman says. "During the whole process, your dog is unconscious and could have irregular breathing. Breathing returns to normal once the seizure ends."

To obtain a diagnosis, your veterinarian will run several tests — bloodwork, urinalysis, toxin scan, liver and thyroid function — to pinpoint or rule out other causes. Your veterinarian also may refer your dog to a veterinary neurologist for Magnetic Resonance Imaging or a Computerized Tomography scan of the brain, an analysis of spinal fluid and an electroencephalogram.

Although there is no cure for idiopathic epilepsy, in most cases the disease can be managed. "The most common drugs used to treat epilepsy are the anti-seizure drugs phenobarbital and potassium bromide," Zinderman says. "These are sometimes used in combination and must be adjusted for each patient. Some medications may make your pet drowsy, but this should not restrict his activity. But not all patients are treated with medication. If your dog's seizures are mild and don't occur more than once every few months, treatment may not be necessary."

Prevention is the best guarantee against serious health problems. Regularly take your Beagle to the veterinarian, and keep an eye out for abnormalities.

HYPOTHYROIDISM

Hypothyroidism is a dysfunction of the thyroid gland resulting in a deficiency of thyroid hormones, specifically tetraiodothyronine or thyroxine (T4) and/or triiodothyronine (T3). Classic signs of hypothyroidism are varied and include weight gain; poor skin and hair coat; smelly ears or coat; lethargy or excitability; food or flea allergy; dry eye syndrome; anemia; mild, chronic dysfunction of the kidney, pancreas, liver or adrenal glands; seizures; muscle weakness; reproductive failure; bleeding tendency; and behavioral change.

The disease also presents itself in the early stages, but many people miss the signs. "The animals can be become thin and maintain a normal hair coat, or sometimes become behaviorally bizarre — aggressive, submissive, phobic, schizophrenic, etc.," says W. Jean Dodds, D.V.M., president of Hemopet, a nonprofit animal blood bank in California. "They can become forgetful or have a short attention span. They can wear a sort of tragic expression where they look worried all the time, or look sad or old."

Dodds says these early-stage changes occur either abruptly or over several months. These changes may be traceable to a specific event, such as producing a litter of puppies, putting the dog on a new medication or having received recent vaccinations. "Sometimes that's just the final thing that puts the animal over the edge," she says.

Onset of hypothyroidism usually occurs after puberty, and Beagles seem to have a high incidence of the disease. Although a transient form of hypothyroidism can occasionally occur in conjunction with another disease or with drugs, most of the time hypothyroidism is triggered by an autoimmune disease.

Autoimmune disease occurs when the body undergoes some kind of immunologic stress or challenge, such as a hormonal imbalance; drug, chemical or toxin exposure; recent vaccinations; or infectious disease. This causes the immune system of a genetically susceptible individual to raise antibodies against the patient's own tissues. In other words, the patient's body literally stops tolerating one or more of its own tissues, eventually causing antibodies to be raised, which will damage those tissues.

Diagnosis of hypothyroidism is made by blood tests that measure circulating bound and unbound (free) thyroid hormone levels, the body's own stimulating hormone level and the presence of autoantibodies against the thyroid proteins, such as the thryoglobulin autoantibody and circulating T3 or T4 autoantibodies.

Although not curable, hypothyroidism can almost always be controlled with treatment. Usually twice-daily thyroid hormone replacements are recommended for the remainder of the dog's life, along with regular annual or semiannual monitoring to ensure the dosage remains effective.

Because hypothyroidism usually indicates the presence of underlying autoimmune disease, Dodds also recommends that owners attempt to minimize the risk of triggering other inappropriate immune responses.

"We need to treat these animals very carefully to avoid overstimulating the immune system," Dodds explains. "Instead of vaccinating them every year once they are adults, we should do serum antibody titers. We should stop overvaccinating puppies with every combination, the so-called 'combo-wombo.' There are so many vaccines in the mixtures today that are not really essential, clinically.

"In areas with low risk for heartworm disease and/or fleas, you don't need to give all these chemical preventives," Dodds adds. Loading the animal's body up with chemicals on a regular basis increases the risk of adverse immunologic or toxic reactions in susceptible dogs. Feed them healthy diets that don't contain chemical preservatives or other kinds of chemicals. Also, keep animals away from chemically treated bushes and grass because they can absorb these chemicals through their noses and feet."

CHERRY EYE

Glandular hypertrophy, or cherry eye, is a condition that occurs when the tear gland on the inner surface of the third eyelid enlarges because of infection. As it swells, it is forced out from beneath the lid, exposing a red growth in the corner of the eye. This condition is commonly seen in Beagles and several other breeds.

The gland of the third eyelid is responsible for about 30 percent of a dog's tear production — important for keeping the dog's cornea lubricated, clean and free of dust — surgical removal of the gland is not recommended.

"We used to remove the gland, but found that later in life dogs would develop a dry eye problem," says Lila Miller, D.V.M., veterinary advisor and senior director of animal science for the American Society of the Prevention of Cruelty to Animals. "The newer procedure is to reposition the gland surgically and tack it in place. With surgical treatment, prognosis is great."

Occasionally, ophthalmic ointment containing antibiotics and steroids will reduce the swelling and keep the gland from becoming infected, but it doesn't offer a permanent solution and reoccurrence of the condition is likely.

CHRONIC HIP DYSPLASIA

Chronic hip dysplasia results in a loose hip joint and abnormal rubbing of the joint surfaces. The joint eventually becomes inflamed, causing chronic pain and even the development of arthritis. The most common heritable orthopedic disease in dogs, chronic hip dysplasia is the No. 1 genetic health problem in dogs, and the Beagle is no exception.

Good health starts with a good diet and regular grooming.

Clinical signs of hip dysplasia include limping, difficulty getting up, stiffness, altered gait, struggling to go up stairs or getting into the car and reduced interest in play. Treatment options vary depending upon the symptoms your dog experiences, his age and when he is diagnosis. Conservative treatments for mildly dysplastic dogs include:

■ weight control.

■ prescription diets to help improve your dog's joint function.

■ glucosamine/chondroitin supplements to promote joint health.

■ pain-relief drugs (anti-inflammatories prescribed under veterinary supervision).

■ regular exercise to maintain muscle tone, strength and range of motion in the joint.

Prognosis varies, depending upon treatment options and the severity of the disease. Mildly affected dogs can often be successfully managed with conservative treatments for a long time. The outlook for hip repair and reconstruction generally ranges from good to excellent.

Although hip dysplasia is a genetic disorder, other causes include overfeeding and over- or under-supplementation of carbohydrates, calcium and phosphorous in growing dogs. Talk with your veterinarian to find the appropriate diet formula for your puppy or adolescent dog.

OTHER HEALTH CONCERNS

Airborne allergies: Just as humans suffer from hay fever during allergy season, many dogs suffer from the same. When the pollen count is high, your Beagle might suffer, but don't expect him to sneeze or have a runny nose like a human. Beagles react to pollen allergies in the same way they react to fleas; they scratch and bite themselves. Dogs, like humans, can be tested for allergens. Be sure to discuss allergy testing with your vet.

Autoimmune illness: An autoimmune illness is one in which the immune system overacts and does not recognize parts of the affected person. Instead, the immune system starts to react as if these parts were foreign cells and need to be destroyed. An example of an autoimmune illness is rheumatoid arthritis, which occurs when the body does not recognize the joints. This leads to a very painful and damaging reaction in the joints. Rheumatoid arthritis has nothing to do with age, so it can also occur in puppies. The wear-and-tear arthritis in older people or dogs is called osteoarthritis.

Lupus is another autoimmune disease that affects dogs as well as people. It can take variable forms, affecting the kidneys, bones and skin. It can be fatal, so it is treated with steroids, which have very significant side effects. Steroids calm down the allergic reaction to the body's tissues, which helps the lupus, but also affects the body's reaction to actual foreign cells such as bacteria; it also thins the skin and bones.

Food Allergies: Properly feeding your Beagle is very important. An incorrect diet could affect your dog's health, behavior and nervous system, possibly making a normal dog aggressive. The result of a good or bad diet is most visible in a dog's skin and coat, but internal organs are affected, too.

Dogs are allergic to many foods that are popular and highly recommended by breeders and veterinarians. Changing the brand of food may not eliminate the problem if the ingredient to which your dog is allergic is contained in the new brand.

Recognizing a food allergy can be difficult. Humans often have rashes or swelling of the lips or eyes when they eat foods they are allergic to. Dogs do not usually develop

Regular vet check ups are scheduled by smart owners.

rashes, but they react the same way they do to an airborne allergy or parasite bite; they itch, scratch and bite. While pollen allergies and parasite bites are usually seasonal, food allergies are year-round problems.

Diagnosis of a food allergy is based on a two- to four-week dietary trial with a home-cooked diet, excluding all other foods. The diet should consist of boiled rice or potato with a source of protein that your Beagle has never eaten before, such as fresh or frozen fish, lamb or even something as exotic as pheasant. Water has to be the only drink, and it is important that no other foods are fed during this trial. If your dog's condition improves, try the original diet again to see if the itching resumes. If it does, then your dog is allergic to his original diet. You must find a diet that does not distress your dog's skin. Start with a commercially available hypoallergenic food or the homemade diet that you created for the allergy trial.

In young puppies, roundworms cause bloated bellies, diarrhea and vomiting, and are transmitted from the mother (through blood or milk). Affected pups will not appear as animated as normal puppies. The worms appear spaghetti-like, measuring as long as 6 inches!

Food intolerance is the inability to completely digest certain foods. This occurs because the dog does not have the enzymes necessary to digest some foodstuffs. All puppies have the enzymes needed to digest canine milk, but some dogs do not have the enzymes to digest cow milk, resulting in loose bowels, stomach pains and flatulence.

Dogs often do not have the enzymes to digest soy or other beans. The treatment is to exclude these foods from your Beagle's diet.

EXTERNAL PARASITES

Insect bites itch, erupt and can become infected. Dogs have the same reaction to fleas, ticks and mites. When an insect lands on you, you can whisk it away. Unfortunately, when your Beagle is bitten by a flea, tick or mite, he can only scratch or bite.

By the time your Beagle has been bitten, the parasite has done its damage. It may have laid eggs, which will cause further problems. The itching from parasite bites is probably due to the saliva injected into the site when the parasite sucks the dog's blood.

Fleas: Of all the health and grooming problems to which canines are susceptible, none is better known and more frustrating than fleas. Flea infestation is relatively simple to cure but difficult to prevent.

To control flea infestation, you have to understand the flea's life cycle. Fleas are often thought of as a summertime problem, but centrally heated homes have made fleas a year-round problem. The most effective method of flea control is a two-stage approach: kill the adult fleas, then control the development of pupae (pre-adult) fleas. Unfortunately, no single active ingredient is effective against all stages of the flea life cycle.

Treating fleas should be a two-pronged attack. First, the environment needs to be treated; this includes carpets and furniture, especially your Beagle's bedding and areas underneath furniture. The environment should be treated with a household spray containing an insect growth regulator and an insecticide to kill the adult fleas. Most insecticides are effective against eggs and larvae; they actually mimic the fleas' own hormones and stop the eggs and larvae from developing into adult fleas. There are currently no treatments available to attack the pupae stage of the life cycle, so the adult insecticide is used to kill the newly hatched adult fleas before they find a host. Most insect growth regulators are active for many months, while adult insecticides are only active for a few days.

When treating fleas with a household spray, vacuum before applying the product. This stimulates as many pupae as possible to hatch into adult fleas. The vacuum cleaner should also be treated with an insecticide to prevent the eggs and larvae that have been collected in the vacuum bag from hatching.

The second stage of treatment is to apply an adult insecticide to your Beagle. Traditionally, this would be in the form of a collar or a spray. Recent innovations include digestible insecticides that poison the fleas when they ingest the dog's blood. Alternatively, there are drops that, when placed on the back of the dog's neck, spread throughout the hair and skin to kill adult fleas.

Ticks: Though not as common as fleas, ticks are found all over the tropical and temperate world. They don't bite like fleas; they harpoon. They dig their sharp *proboscis* (nose) into the Beagle's skin and drink the blood, which is their only food and drink. Ticks are controlled the same way fleas are controlled.

The American dog tick, *Dermacentor variabilis*, may be the most common dog tick in many areas, especially those areas where the climate is hot and humid. Most dog ticks have life expectancies of a week to 6 months, depending on climatic conditions. They can neither jump nor fly, but they can crawl slowly and can travel up to 16 feet to reach a sleeping or unsuspecting dog.

Mites: Just as fleas and ticks can be problematic for your dog, mites can also lead to an itch fit. Microscopic in size, mites are related to ticks and generally take up permanent residence on their host animal — in this case, a Beagle. The term "mange" refers to any infestation caused by one of the mighty mites, of which there are six varieties that smart dog owners should know about.

■ Demodex mites cause a condition known as *demodicosis* (sometimes called "red mange" or "follicular mange"), in which the mites live in the dog's hair follicles and sebaceous glands in larger–than–normal numbers. Most dogs recover from this type of mange without any treatment, though topical therapies are commonly prescribed by a veterinarian.

■ The *Cheyletiellosis* mite is the hook-mouthed culprit associated with "walking dandruff," a condition that affects dogs as well as cats and rabbits. If untreated, this mange can affect a whole kennel of dogs and can be spread to humans as well.

■ The *Sarcoptes* mite causes intense itching on the dog in the form of a condition known as scabies or sarcoptic mange. Scabies is highly contagious and can be passed to humans. Sometimes an allergic reaction to the mite worsens the severe itching associated with sarcoptic mange.

■ Ear mites, *Otodectes cynotis*, lead to otodectic mange, which commonly affects the outer ear canal of the dog, though other areas can be affected as well. Your vet can prescribe a treatment to flush out the ears and kill any eggs. A complete month of treatment is necessary to cure this mange.

■ Two other mites, less common in dogs, include *Dermanyssus gallinae* (the "poultry" or "red" mite) and *Eutrombicula alfreddugesi* (the North American mite associated with trombiculidiasis or chigger infestation). The types of mange caused by both of these mites must be treated by vets.

INTERNAL PARASITES

Most animals — fish, birds and mammals, including dogs and humans — have worms and other parasites that live inside their bodies. According to Dr. Herbert R. Axelrod, a fish pathologist, there are two kinds of parasites: "smart" and "dumb." The smart parasites live in peaceful cooperation with their hosts — a symbiotic relationship — while the dumb parasites kill their hosts. Most worm infections are relatively easy to control. If they are not controlled, they weaken the host dog to the point that other medical problems occur, but they do not kill the host as dumb parasites would.

Roundworms: Roundworms live in the dog's intestines and continually shed eggs. It has been estimated that a dog produces about six or more ounces of feces every day; each ounce averages hundreds of thousands of roundworm eggs. There are no known areas in which dogs roam that do not contain roundworm eggs. Because roundworms infect people, too, it is wise to have your dog regularly tested.

Roundworm infection can kill puppies and cause severe problems in adult dogs, as the hatched larvae travel to the lungs and trachea through the bloodstream. Cleanliness is the best prevention against roundworms. Always pick up after your dog and dispose of feces in appropriate receptacles.

Hookworms: Hookworms are dangerous to humans as well as to dogs and cats, and can be the cause of severe iron-deficiency anemia. The worm uses its teeth to attach itself to the dog's intestines and changes the site of its attachment about six times per day. Each time the worm repositions itself, the dog loses blood and can become anemic.

Symptoms of hookworm infection include dark stools, weight loss, general weakness, pale coloration and anemia, as well as possible skin problems. Fortunately, hookworms are easily purged with a number of medications that have proven effective. Discuss these with your veterinarian. Most heartworm preventives include a hookworm insecticide.

Humans, can be infected by hookworms through exposure to contaminated feces. Because the worms cannot complete their life cycle on a human, the worms simply infest the skin and cause irritation. As a preventive, use disposable gloves or a poop scoop to pick up your Beagle's droppings and prevent your dog (or neighborhood cats) from defecating in children's play areas.

Tapeworms: There are many species of tapeworms, all of which are carried by fleas. Fleas are so small that your Beagle could pass them onto your hands, your plate or your food, making it possible for you to ingest a flea that is carrying tapeworm eggs. While a tapeworm infection is not life-threatening in dogs (it's a *smart* parasite!), if transmitted to humans, it can be the cause of a serious liver disease.

Whipworms: In North America, whipworms are counted among the most common parasitic worms in dogs. Affected dogs may only experience upset tummies, colic and diarrhea. These worms, however, can live for months or years in the dog, beginning their larval stage in the small intestine, spending their adult life in the large intestine and finally passing infective eggs through the dog's feces. The only way to detect whipworms is through a fecal examination, though this is not always foolproof. Treatment for whipworms is tricky, due to the worms' unusual life cycle, and often dogs are reinfected due to exposure to infective eggs on the ground. Cleaning up droppings in your backyard and in public places is necessary for sanitary purposes and the health of your dog and others.

Threadworms: Though less common than roundworms, hookworms and the aforementioned parasites, threadworms concern dog owners in the southwestern United States and the Gulf Coast area where the climate is hot and humid, which is the prime environment for threadworms. Living in the small intestine of the dog, this worm measures a mere two millimeters and is round in shape. Like the whipworm, the threadworm's life cycle is very complex and the eggs and larvae are transported through the feces.

A deadly disease in humans, threadworms readily infect people, mostly through the handling of feces. Threadworms are most often seen in young puppies. The most common symptoms include bloody diarrhea and pneumonia. Infected puppies must be promptly isolated and treated to prevent spreading the threadworms to other dogs and humans; vets recommend a follow-up treatment one month later.

Heartworms: Heartworms are thin, extended worms that measure up to 12 inches long and live in a dog's heart and inhabit the major blood vessels around it. Dogs may have up to 200 heartworms. Symptoms may be loss of energy, loss of appetite, coughing, the development of a pot belly and anemia.

Heartworms are transmitted by mosquitoes, which drink the blood of infected dogs and take in larvae with the blood. The larvae, called *microfilariae*, develop within the body of the mosquito and are then passed on to the next dog bitten after the larvae mature.

It takes two to three weeks for the larvae to develop to the infective stage within the body of the mosquito. Dogs are usually treated at about 6 weeks of age and are maintained on a prophylactic dose given monthly to regulate proliferation.

Blood testing for heartworms is not necessarily indicative of how seriously your dog is infected. Although this is a dangerous disease, it is difficult for a dog to be infected. Discuss the various preventives with your vet, because there are many different types now available. Together you can decide on a safe course of prevention for your dog.

FOOD GUIDE

You have probably heard it a thousand times: You are what you eat. Believe it or not, it is very true. For dogs, they are what you feed them because they have little choice in the matter. Even smart owners, who want to feed their Beagles the best, often cannot do so because it can be so confusing. With the overwhelming assortment of dog foods available, it's difficult to figure out which one is truly best for their dogs.

BASIC TYPES

Dog foods are produced in various types: dry, wet (canned), semimoist and frozen.

Dry food is useful for cost-conscious owners because it is usually less expensive than the others. These foods also contain the least fat and the most preservatives. Dry food is bulky and takes longer to eat than other foods, so it's more filling.

Some dry foods for small dogs have compositions that are identical to those for larger dogs, but the kibble is smaller and easier to chew. Small dogs don't really need smaller kibble, though your dog may prefer it. Many small dogs eat standard-size kibble with no trouble at all.

it's a **Fact**

Bones can cause gastro-intestinal obstruction and perforation, and may be contaminated with salmonella or E. coli. Leave them in the trash and give your dog a nylon bone toy instead.

Wet food — available in cans or foil pouches — is usually 60 to 70 percent water and is more expensive than dry food. A palatable source of concentrated nutrition, wet food also makes a good supplement for underweight dogs or those recovering from illnesses. Some smart owners add a little wet food to dry food to increase its appeal.

Semimoist food is flavorful, but it usually contains lots of sugar. That can lead to dental problems and obesity. Therefore, semi-moist food is not a good choice for your Beagle's main diet.

Frozen food, which is available in cooked and in raw forms, is usually more expensive than wet foods. The advantages of frozen food are similar to those of wet foods.

The amount of food that your Beagle needs depends on a number of factors, such as his age, activity level, the quality of the food, reproductive status (if your Beagle is a female) and size. What's the easiest way to figure it out? Start with the manufacturer's recommended amount, then adjust it according to your dog's response. For example, feed the recommended amount for a few weeks, and if your Beagle loses weight, increase the amount by 10 to 20 percent. If your hound gains weight, decrease the amount. It won't take long to determine the amount of food that keeps your best friend in optimal condition.

NUTRITION 101

All Beagles (and all dogs, for that matter) need proteins, carbohydrates, fats, vitamins and minerals to be in peak condition.

■ **Proteins** are used for growth and repair of muscles, bones and other tissues. They're also used for the production of antibodies, enzymes and hormones. All dogs need protein, but it's especially important for puppies because they grow and develop so quickly. Protein sources include various types of meat, meat meal, meat byproducts, eggs, dairy products and soybeans.

■ **Carbohydrates** are metabolized into glucose, the body's principal energy source. Carbohydrates are available as sugars, starches and fiber.

• Sugars (simple carbohydrates) are not suitable nutrient sources for dogs.

• Starches — a preferred carbohydrate in dog food — are found in a variety of plant products. Starches must be cooked in order to be digested.

• Fiber (cellulose) — also a preferred type of carbohydrate found in dog food — isn't digestible, but helps the digestive tract function properly.

Treats should only account for 10 percent of your dog's regular diet.

Believe it or not, during your Beagle's lifetime, you'll buy a few thousand pounds of dog food! Go to **DogChannel.com/Club-Beagle** and download a chart that outlines the cost of dog food.

A healthy dog needs access to plenty of fresh, clean water all day long.

■ **Fats** are also a source of energy and play an important role in maintaining your Beagle's skin and coat health, hormone production, nervous system function and vitamin transport. However, you must be aware of the fact that fats increase the palatability and the calorie count of dog food, which can lead to serious health problems, such as obesity, for puppies or dogs who are allowed to overindulge. Some foods contain added amounts of omega fatty acids such as docosahexaenoic acid, a compound that may enhance brain development and learning in puppies but is not considered an essential nutrient by the Association of American Feed Control Officials (www.aafco.org). Fats used in dog foods include tallow, lard, poultry fat, fish oil and vegetable oils.

■ **Vitamins** and **minerals** are essential to dogs for proper muscle and nerve function, bone growth, healing, metabolism and fluid balance. Especially important for your Beagle puppy are calcium, phosphorus and vitamin D, which must be supplied in the right balance to ensure proper development and maintenance of bones and teeth.

Just as your dog receives proper nutrition from his food, water essential, as well. Water keeps your dog's body hydrated and facilitates normal function of the body's systems. During housetraining, it is necessary to keep an eye on how much water your Beagle is drinking, but once he is reliably trained, he should have access to clean, fresh water at all times, especially if you feed him dry food. Make sure that your dog's water bowl is clean, and change the water often.

CHECK OUT THE LABEL

To help you get a feel for what you are feeding your dog, start by taking a look at the label on the package or can. Look for the words "complete and balanced." This tells

Dogs of all ages love treats and table food, but these goodies can unbalance your Beagle's diet and lead to a weight problem if you don't feed him wisely. Table food, whether fed as a treat or as part of a meal, shouldn't account for more than 10 percent of your dog's daily caloric intake. If you plan to give your Beagle treats, be sure to include "treat calories" when calculating his daily food requirement — so you don't end up with a pudgy pup!

When shopping for packaged treats, look for ones that provide complete nutrition. They're basically dog food in a fun form. Choose crunchy goodies for chewing fun and dental health. Other ideas for tasty treats include:

✓ small chunks of cooked, lean meat
✓ dry dog food morsels
✓ cheese
✓ veggies (cooked, raw or frozen)
✓ breads, crackers or dry cereal
✓ unsalted, unbuttered, plain, popped popcorn

Some foods, however, can be dangerous or even deadly to a dog. The following can cause digestive upset (vomiting or diarrhea) or fatal toxic reactions:

✗ **avocados:** if eaten in sufficient quantity these can cause gastrointestinal irritation, with vomiting and diarrhea

✗ **baby food:** may contain onion powder; does not provide balanced nutrition

✗ **chocolate:** contains methylxanthines and theobromine, caffeine-like compounds that can cause vomiting, diarrhea, heart abnormalities, tremors, seizures and death. Darker chocolates contain higher levels of the toxic compounds.

✗ **eggs, raw:** Whites contain an enzyme that prevents uptake of biotin, a B vitamin; may contain salmonella.

✗ **garlic (and related foods):** can cause gastrointestinal irritation and anemia if eaten in sufficient quantity

✗ **grapes:** can cause kidney failure if eaten in sufficient quantity (the toxic dose varies from dog to dog)

✗ **macadamia nuts:** can cause vomiting, weakness, lack of coordination and other problems

✗ **meat, raw:** may contain harmful bacteria such as salmonella or E. coli

✗ **milk:** can cause diarrhea in some puppies

✗ **onions (and related foods):** can cause gastrointestinal irritation and anemia if eaten in sufficient quantity

✗ **raisins:** can cause kidney failure if eaten in sufficient quantity (the toxic dose varies from dog to dog)

✗ **yeast bread dough:** can rise in the gastrointestinal tract, causing obstruction; produces alcohol as it rises

you that the food meets specific nutritional requirements set by the AAFCO for either adults ("maintenance") or puppies and pregnant/lactating females ("growth and reproduction"). The label must state the group for which the food is intended. If you're feeding a puppy, choose a "growth and reproduction" food.

The nutrition label also includes a list of minimum protein, minimum fat, maximum fiber and maximum moisture content. (You won't find carbohydrate content because it's everything that isn't protein, fat, fiber and moisture.)

The nutritional analysis refers to crude protein and crude fat — amounts that have been determined in the laboratory. This analysis is technically accurate, but it does not tell you anything about digestibility: how much of the particular nutrient your Beagle can actually use. For information about digestibility, contact the manufacturer (check the label for a telephone number and website address).

Virtually all commercial puppy foods exceed AAFCO's minimal requirements for protein and fat, the two nutrients most commonly evaluated when comparing foods.

Protein levels in dry puppy foods usually range from about 26 to 30 percent; for canned foods, the values are about 9 to 13 percent. The fat content of dry puppy foods is about 20 percent or more; for canned foods, it's 8 percent or more. (Dry food values are larger than canned food values because dry food contains less water; the values are actually similar when compared on a dry matter basis.)

Finally, check the ingredients on the label, which lists the ingredients in descending order by weight. Manufacturers are allowed to list separately different forms of a single ingredient (e.g., ground corn and corn gluten meal). The food may contain meat byproducts, meat and bone meal, and animal fat, which probably won't appeal to you but are nutritious and safe for your puppy. Higher quality foods usually have meat or meat products near the top of the ingredient list, but you don't need to worry about grain products as long as the label indicates that the food is nutritionally complete. Dogs are omnivores (not carnivores, as commonly believed), so all balanced dog foods contain animal and plant ingredients.

STORE IT RIGHT

Properly storing your Beagle's food will ensure that it maintains its quality, nutrient content and taste. Here's what you should do before and after you open that package or can.

◆ Dry food should be stored in a cool, dry, bug- and vermin-free environment, espe-

Did You Know?

If you're feeding a puppy food that's complete and balanced, your young Beagle doesn't need any dietary supplements such as vitamins, minerals or other types of food. In fact, dietary supplements could even harm your puppy by unbalancing his diet. If you have questions about supplementing your Beagle's diet, ask your veterinarian.

cially if it's a preservative-free product. Many manufacturers include an expiration date on the package label, but this usually refers to the shelf life of the unopened package. For optimal quality, don't buy more dry food than your Beagle can eat in one month. To store dry food after opening the bag, fold down the bag's top several times and secure it with a clip or empty the contents into a food-grade airtight plastic container (available at pet-supply stores or discount stores). Make sure the storage container is clean and dry and has never been used to store toxic materials; the residue can be harmful if ingested by your dog.

◆ Canned food, if unopened, can remain good for three years or longer, but it's best to use it within one year of purchase. Discard puffy cans or those that are leaking fluid. Leftover canned food should be covered and refrigerated, then used within three days.

◆ Frozen food can be stored for at least one year in the freezer. Longer storage can cause deterioration of the quality and taste of the food. Thaw frozen food in the refrigerator or use the defrost setting of your microwave. Cover and refrigerate leftovers, which should be used within 24 hours.

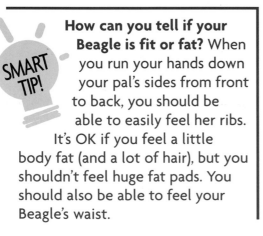

How can you tell if your Beagle is fit or fat? When you run your hands down your pal's sides from front to back, you should be able to easily feel her ribs. It's OK if you feel a little body fat (and a lot of hair), but you shouldn't feel huge fat pads. You should also be able to feel your Beagle's waist.

SMART TIP!

STAGES OF LIFE

When selecting your dog's diet, three stages of development must be considered: the puppy stage, the adult stage and the senior stage.

Puppy Diets: Pups instinctively want to nurse, and a normal puppy will exhibit this behavior from just a few moments following birth. Puppies should be allowed to nurse for about the first six weeks, although by the third or fourth week, the breeder should begin to introduce small portions of suitable solid food. Most breeders like to initially introduce alternate milk and solid-food meals, leading up to weaning time.

By the time Beagle puppies are 7 weeks old (or a maximum of 8), they should be fully weaned and fed solely on puppy food. Selection of the most suitable, high-quality food at this time is essential because a

Your puppy deserves the very best when it comes to his health and care. Read all food labels carefully to ensure that you're feeding him the best foods possible.

puppy's fastest growth rate is during the first year of life. Seek advice about your dog's diet from your veterinarian. The frequency of meals will be reduced over time, and when a young dog has reached 10 to 12 months, he should be switched to an adult diet.

Puppy and junior diets can be well balanced for the needs of your Beagle so that additional vitamin, mineral and protein supplements will not be required.

How often should you feed your Beagle in a day? Puppies have small stomachs and high metabolism, so they need to eat several times a day to consume sufficient nutrients. If your Beagle puppy is younger than 3 months old, feed him four or five meals a day. When your Beagle is 3 to 5 months old, decrease the number of meals to three or four. At 6 months, most puppies can move to an adult schedule of two meals a day.

Adult Diets: A dog is considered an adult when he has stopped growing. Rely on your veterinarian or canine dietary specialist to recommend an acceptable maintenance diet. Major dog food manufacturers specialize in this type of food, and smart owners must select the one best suited to their dogs' needs. Do not leave food out all day for "free-choice" feeding, as this freedom inevitably translates to inches around your dog's waist.

Senior Diets: As dogs get older, their metabolism begins to change. A senior Beagle usually exercises less, moves more slowly and sleeps more.

This change in his lifestyle and physiological performance requires a change in diet. Because these changes take place slowly, they might not be recognizable at first. These metabolic changes increase the tendency toward obesity, requiring an even more vigilant approach to feeding. Obesity in an older dog exacerbates the health problems that already accompany old age.

As a Beagle ages, few of his organs function up to par. The kidneys slow down, and the intestines become less efficient. These age-related factors are best handled with a change in diet and a change in feeding schedule to give smaller portions that are more easily digested.

There is no single best diet for an older Beagle. While many older dogs will do perfectly fine on light or senior diets, other dogs will do better on special premium diets such as lamb and rice. Be sensitive to your senior Beagle's diet, and this will help control other problems that may arise with your old friend.

When you go grocery shopping, purchase some healthy snacks for your Beagle, like low-fat cheese you can crumble, mini hot dogs or even fresh veggies like baby carrots!

These delicious, dog-friendly recipes will have your furry friend smacking her lips and salivating for more. Just remember: Treats aren't meant to replace your dog's regular meals. Give your Beagle snacks sparingly and continue to feed her nutritious, well-balanced meals.

Cheddar Squares

$\frac{1}{3}$ cup all-natural applesauce
$\frac{1}{3}$ cup low-fat cheddar cheese, shredded
$\frac{1}{3}$ cup water
2 cups unbleached white flour

In a medium bowl, mix all the wet ingredients. In a large bowl, mix the flour. Slowly add all the wet ingredients to the flour.
Mix well. Pour batter into a greased, 13x9x2-inch pan. Bake at 375-degrees Fahrenheit for 25 to 30 minutes. Bars are done when a toothpick inserted in the center and comes out clean when removed. Cool and cut into bars. This recipe makes about 54, $1\frac{1}{2}$-inch bars.

Peanut Butter Bites

3 tablespoons vegetable oil
$\frac{1}{4}$ cup smooth peanut butter, no salt or sugar
$\frac{1}{4}$ cup honey
$1\frac{1}{2}$ teaspoon baking powder
2 eggs
2 cups whole wheat flour

In a large bowl, mix all ingredients until dough is firm. If the dough is too sticky, mix in a small amount of flour. Knead dough on a lightly floured surface until firm. Roll out dough half an inch thick, and cut with cookie cutters. Put cookies on a cookie sheet half an inch apart. Bake at 350-degrees Fahrenheit for 20 to 25 minutes. When done, cookies should be firm to the touch. Turn oven off and leave cookies for one to two hours to harden. This recipe makes about 40, 2-inch-long cookies.

GROOMING

BASICS

As an all-around hound — loyal, happy, easygoing and high on the cuteness quotient — there is nothing *fancy* about the Beagle. An easy-keeper, this little canine character with his compact size and easy-to-care-for coat fits in, literally, almost anywhere.

Befitting of a hunting dog, the Beagle's coat is medium length, dense and weatherproof. Wearing a double coat, the breed is virtually waterproof. After a romp in the rain or a dip in the stream, a good shake is all a Beagle needs to dry off. His hard outer coat serves as body armor in the breed's hunting pursuits through brambles and brush, and the soft undercoat insulates the dog against the cold.

A quality Beagle coat should feel hard to the touch and shine with vitality, according to the American Kennel Club standard. A short, thin coat or one that is too soft would not permit the easy dispersal of water and is considered defective.

Despite the breed's smooth and sleek appearance, Beagles do shed. Sometimes it is not very noticeable because their coat is relatively short. The Beagle's coat is

Did You Know?

Nail clipping can be tricky, so many dog owners leave the task for the professionals. However, if you walk your Beagle on concrete, you may not have to worry about it. The concrete acts like a nail file and should help keep your dog's nails neatly trimmed.

classified as medium in length compared to the truly short coat of a Doberman, for example.

Shedding is more abundant in the spring when Beagles drop their thicker winter coats. Climate changes are not the only cause of shedding: Hair growth is encouraged during the winter when there is less daylight. The breed also "blows coat" during the fall.

TOOLS OF THE TRADE

If you're starting with a Beagle puppy, daily brushing and grooming will assist in socializing your pup and getting him accustomed to your loving touch. Adult Beagles should be brushed regularly, too. For this task, you'll need to have a few supplies on hand:

■ shampoo and conditioner specifically formulated for dogs

■ medium bristle brush, hound glove, a hand glove or rubber curry brush

■ thin, metal comb

A smart owner's best protection against shedding is weekly brushing to loosen and remove dead hair that would otherwise shed. This will promote new hair growth and lift out small amounts of dirt. When brushing, start at the head and work back to the tail. It's a good idea to time one of your weekly brushing sessions right before your Beagle's monthly bath.

The tools used for brushing are a matter of personal preference. Some owners prefer a thin, metal comb to brush their Beagles because it removes dead hair from the undercoat. Many groomers recommend brushing a Beagle with a hand glove or rubber brush. A hand glove is exactly what it sounds like; you slide it onto your hand with the brush portion facing out from your palm. This is an easy and convenient way to brush your dog.

Keeping your Beagle's nails neatly trimmed will maintain proper spinal alignment and avoid causing him pain.

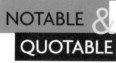

NOTABLE & QUOTABLE *After removing a tick, clean your dog's skin with hydrogen peroxide. If Lyme disease is common where you live, have your veterinarian test the tick. Tick preventive medication will discourage ticks from attaching and kill any that do.*

— groomer Andrea Vilardi from West Paterson, N.J.

KEEN ON CLEAN

Lucky for Beagle owners, the breed is fairly clean: They do not drool or have strong body odor. A bath every two to three months should do just fine. However, since these dogs tend to be happy wanderers — noses seeking out malodorous, delectable substances such as goose manure, animal carcasses or rotting vegetation to roll in — they may require more frequent bathing. For puppies, a mild, tearless shampoo is best; for adults, opt for a deodorizing shampoo, a natural hypoallergenic shampoo or an insecticide shampoo.

Because of his compact size, your Beagle may be bathed right in the sink or tub. Soak the coat all the way through with your shower attachment, then massage in the shampoo. If you are giving a flea bath or a medicated shampoo to treat dry skin, leave the lather on for a full 15 minutes. Then rinse, rinse, rinse! Shampoo residue in the coat will result in a dry, itchy dog.

Towel-dry the dog as thoroughly as possible; then run a fine-toothed flea comb through the coat to catch any dead hairs or dead fleas. A spray of coat conditioner, or show sheen, and your pet is good to go; but letting him outside to run around while damp is not a good idea. Being a Beagle and all, he probably will find another aromatic substance or some plain old mud to roll in, undoing all your good work.

If your Beagle is prone to fleas, try a flea shampoo that naturally kills fleas. Such shampoos are made from citrus, neem, eucalyptus, tea tree oil (melaluca), pennyroyal or citronella, or contain pyrethrins, substances derived from chrysanthemum petals.

If there are fleas on your dog, you can be sure they are also in your house. The solution: a thorough fogging with flea bombs containing insect growth regulators. Fortunately, flea prevention has been revolutionized with the advent of "spot-on" products, which are applied once a month to keep fleas and ticks off your pet. In addition, you can choose from a wide variety of flea collars.

NAILING THINGS DOWN

The best time to clip your dog's nails is immediately after a bath because the water will have softened the nails, and your Beagle may be somewhat tired out by the bath. Nail trimming is recommended every two weeks, using nail clippers or a nail grinding tool.

Trimming nails are crucial to maintaining the Beagle's normal foot shape. Long nails can permanently damage a dog's feet; the tight ligaments of round, arched feet will break down more quickly. If your dog's nails are clicking on the floor, they need trimming.

Your Beagle should be accustomed to having his nails trimmed at an early age because it will be part of your maintenance routine throughout his life. Not only do neatly trimmed nails look nicer, but long nails can unintentionally scratch someone. Also, long nails have a better chance of ripping and bleeding, or causing your Beagle's toes to spread.

Before you start clipping, make sure you can identify the "quick" in each nail (the vein in the center of each nail). It will bleed if accidentally cut, which will be painful for

it's a Fact

Shedding naturally occurs in the spring and fall, and for females, after each estrus (heat) cycle. It also can occur during times of illness, stress and excitement.

Your Beagle has a proud legacy, therefore he should be kept clean and smell fresh all the time.

your dog since it contains a web of nerve endings. Keep some type of clotting agent on hand, such as a styptic pencil or styptic powder (the type used for shaving). This will quickly stop the bleeding when applied to

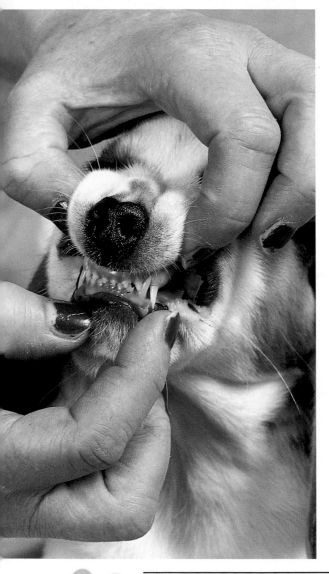

the end of the cut nail. Do not panic if this happens, just stop the bleeding and talk soothingly to your dog. Once he has calmed down, move on to the next nail. It is better to clip a little at a time, particularly with dogs who have dark nails, where the quick isn't easily visible.

Hold your dog steady as you begin trimming his nails; you do not want him to make any sudden movements or run away. Talk to him calmly and stroke him as you clip. Holding his foot in your hand, simply take off the end of each nail in one quick clip. You can purchase nail clippers that are specially made for dogs at pet-supply stores.

There are two predominant types of clippers. One is the guillotine clipper, which is a hole with a blade in the middle. Using this tool, squeeze the handles so that the blade meets the nail and chops it off. It sounds gruesome, and for some dogs, it is utterly intolerable. Scissor-type clippers are gentler on the nail. The important thing to make sure of is that the blades on either of these clippers are sharp. Once you are at the desired length, use a nail file to smooth the rough edges of the nails so they don't catch on carpeting or outdoor debris.

A third option is a cordless nail grinder fitted with a fine grade (100 grit) sandpaper cylinder. Stone cylinders are more prone to heat buildup and vibration. When grinding, use a low speed (5,000 to 10,000 rpm). Hold your dog's paw firmly in one hand spreading the toes slightly apart. Touch the spinning grinder wheel to the nail tip for one or two seconds without applying pressure. Repeat if

Every Beagle deserves to look beautiful. What do you need to keep your Beagle looking his best? Go to Club Beagle (**DogChannel.com/Club-Beagle**) and download a checklist of essential grooming equipment you and your Beagle will need.

JOIN OUR ONLINE Club Beagle™

necessary to remove the nail tip protruding beyond the quick. Grinders have the added benefit of leaving nails smooth and free of sharp, jagged edges traditional nail clippers leave behind.

If the procedure becomes more than you can deal with, just remember: Groomers and veterinarians charge a nominal fee to clip nails. By using their services you won't have to see your pet glower at you for the rest of the night.

When inspecting your dog's paws, you must check not only his nails but also the pads of his paws. Check to see that the pads are not cracked and always inspect between the pads to be sure nothing has become lodged there. Depending upon the season, there may be a danger of grass seeds or thorns becoming embedded, or even tar from the road.

Butter, by the way, is useful in removing tar from your Beagle's paws.

THE EARS HAVE IT

Once your Beagle's feet are neatly trimmed, move on to the ears. Since Beagles have drop ears that hang down, they are

Your Beagle's ears are his trademark. Don't forget to pay attention to them during your grooming routine.

Grooming shouldn't be seen as a chore; instead, it is a wonderful way to bond with your Beagle.

SMART TIP!

A Beagle shouldn't be caught in the middle of a power struggle between children and parents. Divvy up grooming and bathing responsibilities early on, and make the issue non-negotiable.

A clean Beagle is welcomed into the house; a dirty one is banished to the backyard, always on the outside looking in. Even breeds that are low-maintenance, such as Beagles, need some regular grooming.

prone to waxy buildup and ear infections. To help you keep your Beagle's ears clean and preserve the ears' proper pH balance, swab out the ears weekly with a cotton ball or soft tissue soaked in one of the many over-the-counter ear-wash products.

Look way down inside your dog's ears. Do you see a bit of tan wax? That's fine; leave it. Do you see gobs of gunk? That's not OK.

If your Beagle is constantly scratching his ears and shaking his head, take a close look at that gunk. Place some on a piece of black paper and look at it with a magnifying glass. If you see little white moving specks, your dog has ear mites. You'll need a veterinarian to confirm your diagnosis, so that he or she can prescribe a proper and effective treatment that won't damage your dog's ears.

If your Beagle tilts his head and acts like his ear hurts, or if the ear appears red and swollen, it's time to see the veterinarian. You don't want to clean his ears if he's in pain or if there's a chance he might have a perforated eardrum.

Assuming your Beagle just has dirty ears, cleaning them is quite simple. Quickly squeeze some of the cleaning solution into your dog's ear; if you go slowly, the solution will tickle and he'll shake it right out. Keep your hand on the base of the ear, and massage the liquid in so it squishes all around. Your Beagle will shake the liquid out, flinging dissolved gunk all over the place, so you may want to do this outdoors. Wipe clean any goop hanging on the ears with a cotton ball. For really dirty ears, do this several times in the course of a week.

After grooming, reward your Beagle for a job well done with some playtime.

Don't stick cotton swabs into your Beagle's ears. They can irritate the skin, pack gunk more tightly or perforate the eardrum. Don't use powders, which will mix with the moisture and form a hard cake. Don't use hydrogen peroxide either, which will leave the ear moist; and most of all, don't be overzealous in your cleaning. More problems are caused by owners stripping the ears of natural waxes than by neglecting to clean them.

A gentle cleaning once a week helps prevent ear problems. Routine cleaning is a preventive measure; it will not clear up an existing infection and may even make it worse.

IT'S THE TOOTH

Like people, Beagles can suffer from dental disease, so experts recommend regular teeth cleanings. Daily brushing is best, but your dog will benefit from having his teeth brushed a few times a week. The teeth should be white and free of yellowish tartar, and the gums should appear healthy and pink. Gums that bleed easily when you perform dental duties may have gingivitis.

The first thing to know is that your puppy probably isn't going to want your fingers in his mouth. Desensitizing your puppy — getting him to accept that you will be looking at and touching his teeth — is the first step to overcoming his resistance. You can begin this as soon as you get your puppy, with the help of the one thing that motivates dogs the most: food.

For starters, let your puppy lick some chicken, vegetable or beef broth off your finger. Then, dip your finger in broth again, and gently insert your finger in the side of your dog's mouth. Touch his side teeth and gums. Several sessions will get your puppy used to having his mouth touched.

Use a toothbrush made for a dog or a fingertip brush. Hold your dog's mouth with the fingers of one hand, and brush with the other. Use toothpaste formulated for dogs with delectable flavors like poultry and beef. Human toothpaste froths too much and can give your dog an upset stomach. Brush in a circular motion with the brush held at a 45-degree angle to the gum line. Be sure to get the fronts, tops and sides of each tooth.

Check your dog's teeth for signs of plaque, tartar or gum disease, including redness, swelling, foul breath, discolored enamel near the gum line and receding gums. If you see these, immediately take your Beagle to the veterinarian.

THE GREAT OUTDOORS 1: SKUNKS

The scent of a skunk is unmistakable, so there will be little doubt if your Beagle gets sprayed by one. If your dog does get sprayed, immediately check to see if, despite the smell, he's physically OK. If your dog really tangled with a skunk and was scratched, make sure his rabies shot is up-to-date because rabies are a concern with skunks. Next, assess where the majority of the spray hit your dog. If he got blasted in the eyes and nose, a trip to the veterinarian is called for. You can gently wipe around the eyes and nose with a damp cloth, but skunk spray in the eyes should be treated by a veterinarian. As for the special odor, here are some remedies:

■ Enzymatic shampoo designed specifically to get the skunk smell out (available at pet-supply stores).

■ Tomato juice liberally applied to your dog's coat. Let it sit on the coat for at least five minutes, then wash with regular dog shampoo. Repeat several times if needed.

■ Mix one quart of hydrogen peroxide, 1/4-cup baking soda and one teaspoon of liquid soap in a large container. When combined together, this mixture will fizz. Soak your dog's fur, massaging the mixture into your dog's fur. Rinse thoroughly.

THE GREAT OUTDOORS 2: PORCUPINES

Another hazardous animal for a Beagle to encounter is the porcupine. If your Beagle wrangles with a porcupine and gets stuck with quills, use pliers to firmly grab the quill close to the skin and pull. If the quills are deep in the mouth or throat, consult your veterinarian. They may need to put your dog under anesthesia to remove them. If you can safely pull the quills yourself, get antibiotics from your veterinarian as a safety precaution.

REWARD A JOB WELL DONE

Rewarding your Beagle for behaving during grooming is the best way to ensure stress-free grooming. Watching your clean, healthy Beagle race from room to room in sheer joy is your reward for being a caring owner.

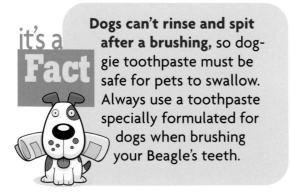

it's a **Fact**

Dogs can't rinse and spit after a brushing, so doggie toothpaste must be safe for pets to swallow. Always use a toothpaste specially formulated for dogs when brushing your Beagle's teeth.

Six Tips for Breed Care

1. Grooming tools can be scary to some dogs, so let yours see and sniff everything at the start. Keep your beauty sessions short, too. Most Beagles don't enjoy standing still for too long.

2. Look at your dog's eyes for any discharge, and her ears for inflammation, debris or foul odor. If you notice anything that doesn't look right, immediately contact your veterinarian.

3. Choose a time to groom your dog when you don't have to rush, and assemble all of the grooming tools before you begin. This way you can focus on your dog's needs instead of having to stop in the middle of the session to search for an item.

4. Start establishing a grooming routine the day after you bring her home. A regular grooming schedule will make it easier to remember what touch-ups your dog needs.

5. Proper nail care helps with your dog's gait and spinal alignment. Nails that are too long can force a dog to walk improperly. Also, nails that are much too long can snag and tear, causing painful injury to your Beagle.

6. Good dental health prevents gum disease and early tooth loss. Brush your Beagle's teeth daily and see a veterinarian yearly.

Six Questions to Ask a Groomer

1. Do you cage dry? Are you willing to hand dry or air dry my pet?

2. What type of shampoo are you using? Is it tearless? If not, do you have a tearless variety available for use?

3. Will you restrain my pet if she acts up during nail clipping? What methods do you use to handle difficult dogs?

4. Are you familiar with the Beagle? Do you have any references from other Beagle owners?

5. Is the shop air-conditioned during hot weather?

6. Will my dog be getting brushed or just bathed?

TRAIN

Reward-based training methods — clicking and luring — instruct dogs on what to do and help them do it correctly, setting them up for success and rewards rather than mistakes and punishment. Positive training not only gets the job done — gets your Beagle to sit, stay, come and heel — it also builds and improves your relationship with your dog.

CLICK THIS

Clicker training is a precise way to mark a desired behavior so your dog knows which behavior earned a reward. A clicker is a small device that makes a sharp clicking sound when a button is pressed. You can purchase them at any pet-supply store. "Charge" the clicker by clicking and giving your Beagle a treat several times until he understands the click means a treat is coming. The click becomes a secondary reinforcer; it's not the reward itself, but it will become closely linked in your dog's mind with a reward, it has the same effect. To use a clicker:

1. Click during the desired behavior, not after your dog has completed it. The

Did You Know? **The prime period for socialization is short.** Most behavior experts agree that positive experiences between 4 and 14 weeks of age are vital to the development of a puppy who'll grow into an adult Beagle with a sound temperament.

timing of the click is crucial to positive training. It's OK if your dog stops the behavior when he hears the click. Once, he's performed the trick, give him the treat afterward; the timing of the treat is not important.

2. Keep treats small and delicious. Small cubes of roast chicken are preferable to a lump of kibble.

3. Click when your dog does anything you like, such as sitting, coming toward you, touching your hand with his nose or raising a paw. These are all easy things your dog is likely to do on his own.

4. Click only once for good behavior. If you want to express enthusiasm, increase the number of treats only.

5. Keep practice sessions short. Fitting a few clicks a day here and there in your normal routine will still bring you results.

6. Correct bad behavior by clicking for good behavior. Click the puppy for relieving himself in the proper spot. Click for paws on the ground, not on the visitors. Instead of scolding for barking, click when your dog is silent. Cure leash pulling by clicking and treating those moments when the leash happens to go slack.

7. Click for voluntary or even accidental movements toward your goal. It's OK to coax or lure your dog into a movement or position, but don't push, pull or hold it.

8. Don't expect perfect behavior. Click and treat for small movements in the right direction. For instance, if you want your dog to sit and he starts to crouch: click. You want him to come when called, and he takes a few steps your way: click.

9. Keep raising your goal. As soon as you receive a good response — when your dog is voluntarily lying down, coming toward you or sitting — start asking for more. Wait a few beats until your dog stays down a little longer, comes a little farther or sits a little faster, then click. This training method is called "shaping" a behavior.

10. When your dog has learned to do something for clicks, he will begin showing you the behavior spontaneously, trying to get you to click. Now is the time to begin offering a cue, such as a word or a hand signal. Start clicking for that behavior if it happens during or after the cue. Begin ignoring the behavior when you haven't given the appropriate cue.

11. Don't order your dog around; clicker training is not about commands. If your dog doesn't respond to a cue, he is not disobeying you; he just hasn't learned the cue. Find more ways to cue him for the desired behavior in easier circumstances.

12. Carry a clicker and catch cute behaviors like cocking the head, chasing the tail or holding up one paw. You can click for many different behaviors, whenever you happen to notice them, without confusing your dog. If you have more than one dog, separate them for training and let them take turns.

13. If you get frustrated during a training session, put the clicker away. Don't mix scolding, leash-jerking and correction training with clicker training; you will lose your dog's confidence in the clicker and perhaps in you.

The most important thing to remember while training your dog is to remain calm and patient.

14. If you are not making progress with a particular behavior, you are probably clicking too late. Accurate timing is important. Get someone else to watch you, and perhaps to click for you a few times.

15. Above all, have fun. Clicker-training is a wonderful way to enrich your relationship with your dog.

REWARDS

Most dogs find food rewards meaningful; Beagles are no exception as they tend to be very food motivated. This works well because positive training relies on using treats, at least initially, to encourage a dog to demonstrate a certain behavior. The treat is then given as a reward. When you reinforce desired behaviors with rewards that are valuable to your dog, you are met with happy cooperation rather than resistance.

Positive reinforcement does not necessarily equal passivity. While you are rewarding your Beagle's desirable behaviors, you must still manage him to be sure he isn't getting rewarded for his undesirable behaviors. Training tools, such as leashes, tethers, baby gates and crates, help keep your dog out of trouble. The use of force-free negative punishment (the dog's behavior makes a good thing go away) helps him realize there are negative consequences for inappropriate behaviors.

LEARNING SOCIAL GRACES

Now that you have done all of the preparatory work and have helped your Beagle get accustomed to his new home and

A smart owner will teach his dog basic obedience. Beagles will catch on quick: they're smarties!

family, it's time for you to have some fun! Socializing your tiny pup gives you the opportunity to show off your new friend, and your Beagle gets to reap the benefits of being an adorable little creature whom people will want to pet and gush over how precious he is.

Your pup's socialization began at the breeder's home, but now it is your responsibility to continue it.Besides getting to know his new family, your puppy should be exposed to other people, animals and situations; but, of course, he must not come into close contact with dogs whom you don't know well until he has had all his vaccinations. This will help him become well adjusted as he grows up and is less prone to being timid or fearful of the new things he will encounter.

The socialization he receives up until he is 12 weeks of age is the most critical, as this is the time when he forms his impressions of the outside world. Be especially careful during the 8- to 10-week period, also known as the "fear period." The interaction he receives during this time should be gentle and reassuring. Lack of socialization can manifest itself in fear and aggression as your Beagle matures. Puppies require a lot of human contact, affection, handling and exposure to other animals to become socialized.

Once your Beagle has received his necessary vaccinations, feel free to take him out and about (on his leash, of course). Walk him around the neighborhood, take him on your daily errands, let people pet him and let him meet other dogs and pets. Make sure to expose your Beagle to different people — men, women, kids, babies, men with beards, teenagers with cell phones or riding skateboards, joggers, shoppers, someone in a wheelchair, a pregnant woman, etc. Make sure your Beagle explores different surfaces like sidewalks, gravel and even a puddle. Positive experience is the key to building confidence. It's up to you to make sure your Beagle safely discovers the world so he will be a calm, confident and well-socialized dog.

It's important that you take the lead in all socialization experiences and never put your pup in a scary or potentially harmful situation. Be mindful of your Beagle's limitations. Fifteen minutes at a public market is fine; two hours at a loud outdoor concert is too much. Meeting vaccinated, tolerant and gentle older dogs is great. Meeting dogs whom

A dog who knows how to sit, stay, lie down, come and heel will surely be a favorite among your friends.

Behaviors are best trained by breaking them down into their simplest components, teaching those and then linking them together to end up with the complete behavior. Keep treats small so you can reward many times without stuffing your Beagle. Remember, don't bore your Beagle; avoid excessive repetition.

you don't know or trust isn't a great idea, especially if they appear very energetic, dominant or fearful. Control the situations in which you place your puppy.

The best way to socialize your puppy to a new experience is to make him think it's the best thing ever. You can do this with a lot of happy talk, enthusiasm and, of course, food. To convince your puppy that almost any experience is a blast, always carry treats. Consider carrying two types — a bag of his puppy chow, which you can give him when introducing him to nonthreatening experiences, and a bag of high-value, mouth-watering treats to give him when introducing him to unfamiliar experiences.

BASIC CUES

All Beagles, regardless of your training goals, need to know at least five basic, good-manner behaviors: sit, down, stay, come and heel. Here are some tips for teaching your Beagle these important cues. Once he gets these down, he can move on to harder tricks.

SIT: Every well-behaved Beagle needs to learn how to sit.

- Hold a treat at the end of your Beagle's nose.
- Move the treat over his head.
- When your dog sits, click a clicker or say "Yes!"
- Feed your dog the treat.
- If your dog jumps up, hold the treat lower. If he backs up, back him into a corner and wait until he sits. Be patient. Keep your clicker handy, and click (or say "Yes!") and treat anytime he offers a sit.
- When he is able to easily offers sits, say "sit" just before he offers, so he can make the association between the word and the behavior. Add the sit cue when you know you can get the behavior. Your dog doesn't know what the word means until you repeatedly associate it with the appropriate behavior.
- When your Beagle sits easily on cue, start using intermittent reinforcement by clicking some sits but not others. At first, click most sits and skip an occasional one (this is a high rate of reinforcement). Gradually make your clicks random.

DOWN: If your Beagle can sit, then he can learn to lie down, too!

- ◆ Have your Beagle sit.
- ◆ Hold the treat in front of his nose. Move

SMART TIP!

If you begin teaching the heel cue by taking long walks and letting your dog pull you along, she may misinterpret this action as acceptable. When you pull back on the leash to counteract her pulling, she will read that tug as a signal to pull even harder!

it down slowly, toward the floor. If he follows all the way down, click and treat.

- ◆ If he gets stuck, move the treat down slowly. Click and treat for small movements downward — moving his head a bit lower, or inching one paw forward. Keep clicking and treating until your Beagle is all the way down. Remember, this method is called "shaping" — rewarding small parts of a behavior until your dog succeeds.
- ◆ If your dog stands as you move the treat toward the floor, have him sit, and move the treat even more slowly downward, shaping with clicks and treats for small, downward movements. If he stands, cheerfully say "Oops!" (which means "Sorry, no treat for that!"), have him sit and try again.
- ◆ If shaping isn't working, sit on the floor with your knee raised. Have your Beagle sit next to you. Place your hand with the treat under your knee and lure him under your leg so he lies down and crawls to follow the treat. Click and treat!
- ◆ When you can lure the down easily, add the verbal cue, wait a few seconds to let your dog process the cue, then lure him down to form the association. Repeat until your Beagle goes down on the verbal cue; then begin using intermittent reinforcement.

STAY: What good are sit and down cues if your dog doesn't stay?

- ▲ Begin this training cue with your Beagle in a sit or down position.

▲ Put the treat in front of your dog's nose and keep it there.

▲ Click and reward your Beagle several times while he is in position, then release him with a cue you will always use to tell him the stay is over. Common release cues are: "all done," "break," "free," "free dog," "at ease" and "OK."

▲ When your Beagle will stay in a sit or down position while you click and treat, add your verbal stay cue. Say "stay," pause for a second or two, click and say "stay" again. Be sure to release with an appropriate cue.

▲ When your Beagle is getting the idea, say "stay," whisk the treat out of sight behind your back, click the clicker and whisk the treat back. Be sure to get it all the way to his nose, so he doesn't jump up. Gradually increase the duration of the stay.

▲ When your Beagle will stay for 15 to 20 seconds, add small distractions: shuffling your feet, moving your arms and taking small hops. Gradually increase the number of distractions. If your Beagle makes mistakes, it means you're adding too much, too fast.

Did You Know? Once your Beagle understands what behavior goes with a specific cue, it is time to start weaning her off the food treats. At first, give a treat after each exercise. Then, start to give a treat only after every other exercise. Mix up times when you offer a food reward and when you only offer praise. This way your dog will never know when she is going to receive food and praise, or only praise.

▲ When he'll stay for 15 to 20 seconds with distractions, gradually add distance. Have your Beagle stay, take a half-step back, click, return and treat. When he'll stay with a half-step, tell him to stay, take a *full* step back, click and return. Always return to your dog to treat after you click, but before you release. If you always return, his stay becomes strong. If you call him to you, his stay gets weaker due to his eagerness to come to you.

COME: A reliable recall — coming when called — can be a challenging behavior to teach. It is possible, however. To succeed, you need to install an automatic response to your "come" cue — one so automatic that your Beagle doesn't even stop to think when he hears it, but will spin on his heels and charge toward you at full speed.

■ Start by charging a come cue the same way you charged your clicker. If your Beagle already ignores the word "come," pick a different cue, like "front" or "hugs." Say your cue and feed him a bit of scrumptious treat. Repeat this until his eyes light up when he hears the cue. Now you're ready to start training.

■ With your Beagle on a leash, run away several steps and cheerfully call out your charged cue. When he follows, click the clicker. Feed him a treat when he reaches you. For a more enthusiastic come, run away at full speed as you call him. When he follows at a gallop, stop running, click and give him a treat. The better your Beagle gets at coming, the farther away he can be when you call him.

■ Once your Beagle understands the come cue, play with more people, each holding a clicker and treats. Stand a short distance apart and take turns calling and running away. Click and treat in turn as he comes to each of you. Gradually increase the

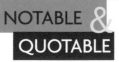 **NOTABLE & QUOTABLE**

If you want to make your dog happy, create a digging spot where she's allowed to disrupt the earth. Encourage her to dig there by burying bones and toys, and helping her dig them up. — Pat Miller, a certified dog trainer and owner of Peaceable Paws dog-training facility in Hagerstown, Md.

Teaching your dog to heel is an important cue during walks, just in case he meets another dog or is tempted to chase after a person or animal.

distance until he comes flying to each person from a distance.

■ When you and your Beagle are ready to practice in wide-open spaces, attach a long line (a 20- to 50-foot leash) to your dog, so you can get a hold of him if that taunting squirrel nearby is too much of a temptation. Then, head to a practice area where there are less tempting distractions.

HEEL: Heeling means that your dog can calmly walk beside you without pulling. It takes time and patience on your part to succeed at teaching your dog that you will not proceed unless he is walking beside you with ease. Pulling out ahead on the leash is definitely unacceptable.

● Begin by holding the leash in your left hand as your Beagle sits beside your left leg. Move the loop end of the leash to your right hand but keep your left hand short on the leash so it keeps your dog close to you.

● Say "heel" and step forward on your left foot. Keep your Beagle close to you and take three steps. Stop and have your dog sit next to you in what we now call the heel position. Praise verbally, but do not touch your dog. Hesitate a moment and begin again with "heel," taking three steps and stopping, at which point your dog is told to sit again.

Your goal here is to have your dog walk those three steps without pulling on the leash. Once he will walk calmly beside you for three steps without pulling, increase the number of steps you take to five. When he will walk politely beside you while you take five steps, you can increase the length of your walk to 10 steps. Keep increasing the length of your stroll until your dog will walk beside you without pulling for as long as you want him to heel. When you stop heeling, indicate to the dog that the exercise is over by petting him and saying "OK, good dog." The "OK" is used as a release word, meaning that the exercise is finished, and he is free to relax.

● If you are dealing with a Beagle who insists on pulling you around, simply put on your brakes and stand your ground until your Beagle realizes that the two of you are not going anywhere until he is beside you and moving at your pace, not his. It may take some time just standing there to convince your dog that you are the leader, and you will be the one to decide on the direction and speed of your travel.

● Each time your dog looks up at you or slows down to give a slack leash between the two of you, quietly praise him and say, "Good heel. Good dog." Eventually, your Beagle will begin to respond, and within a few days he will be walking politely beside you without pulling on the leash. At first, the training sessions should be short and very positive; soon your Beagle will be able to walk nicely with you for increasingly longer distances. Remember to give your Beagle free time and the opportunity to run and play when you have finished heel practice.

LEAVE IT ALONE

Beagles enjoy eating, which makes it easy to train them using treats. But there's a downside to their gastronomic gusto — some Beagles will gobble down anything even remotely edible. This could include fresh food, rotten food, things that once were food and any item that's ever been in contact

SMART TIP!

If your Beagle refuses to sit with both haunches squarely beneath her and instead sits on one side or the other, she may have a physical reason for doing so. Discuss the habit with your veterinarian to be certain your dog isn't suffering from a structural or alignment problem.

with food. So, if you don't want your Beagle gulping down trash, teach him to leave things alone when told.

Place a tempting treat on the floor and cover it with your hand (gloved against teeth, if necessary). Say your cue word ("leave it" or "nah"). Your dog might lick, nibble and paw at your hand; don't give in to him, or you'll reward his bad manners.

Wait until he moves away, then click or praise, and give him a treat. Do not let your dog eat the food that's on the floor, only the treats you give him. Repeat until your Beagle stops moving toward the tempting food.

Lift your hand momentarily, letting your dog see the temptation. Say the cue word. Be ready to protect the treat but instantly reward him if he resists temptation. Repeat, moving your hand farther away and waiting longer before clicking and rewarding.

Gradually increase the difficulty of the cue by practicing in different locations, adding new temptations and dropping treats from standing height.

NOTABLE & QUOTABLE

Be careful in the timing of your treats. A common mistake is to reward your dog at the wrong time. If you reach in your pocket for a food treat and your dog gets up, do not give a treat. Otherwise, she will interpret your reaching in your pocket for complying with the stay cue. — Judy Super, a professional dog trainer in Minneapolis, Minn.

Remember to use your cue word, so your dog will know what he's expected to do. Always reward good behavior! Rehearse this skill daily for a week. After that, you'll have enough real-life opportunities to practice the cue until your Beagle will be able to perform it perfectly.

TRAINING TIPS

If not properly socialized and trained, even a well-bred Beagle will exhibit bad conduct such as jumping up, barking, chasing, chewing and other destructive behaviors. You can prevent these habits and help your Beagle become the perfect dog you've wished for by following some basic training and behavior guidelines.

■ **Be consistent.** Consistency is important, not just in terms of what you allow your Beagle to do (get on the sofa, perhaps) and not do (jump up on people), but also in the verbal and body language cues you use with your dog and in his daily routine.

■ **Be gentle but firm.** Positive training methods are very popular. Properly applied, dog-friendly methods are wonderfully effective at creating canine-human relationships based on respect and cooperation.

■ **Manage behavior.** All living things — especially dogs — repeat behaviors that are rewarded. Behaviors that aren't reinforced will go away.

■ **Provide adequate exercise.** A tired Beagle is a well-behaved Beagle. Give your dog plenty of exercise to avoid problems.

THE THREE-STEP PROGRAM

Perhaps it's too late to give your dog consistency, training and management from the start. Maybe he came from a Beagle rescue shelter or you didn't realize the importance of these basic guidelines when he was a puppy. He already may have learned some bad behaviors. Perhaps they're even part of your Beagle's genetic package. Many problems can be modified with ease using the following three-step process for changing an unwanted behavior.

Step No. 1: Visualize the behavior you want your dog to exhibit. If you simply try to stop your Beagle from doing something, you leave a behavior vacuum. You need to fill that vacuum with something, so your dog doesn't return to the same behavior or fill it with one that's even worse! If you're tired of your dog jumping up, decide what you'd prefer instead. A dog who greets people by sitting politely in front of them is a joy to own.

Step No. 2: Prevent your Beagle from being rewarded for the behavior you don't want him to exhibit. Management to the rescue! When your Beagle jumps up to greet you or get your attention, turn your back and step away to show him that jumping up no longer works in gaining your attention.

Step No. 3: Generously reinforce the desired behavior. Keep in mind that dogs will repeat behaviors that generate rewards. If your Beagle no longer gets attention for jumping up and is heavily reinforced with attention and treats for sitting, he will offer sits instead of jumping, because he's learned that sitting will get him what he wants.

COUNTER-CONDITIONING

The three-step process helps to correct those behaviors that temporarily gives your Beagle satisfaction. For example, he jumps up to get attention; he countersurfs because he finds good food on counters; he nips at your hands to get you to play with him.

The steps don't work well when you're dealing with behaviors that are based in strong emotion, such as aggression and fear, or with hardwired behaviors such as chasing prey. With these, you can change the emotional or hardwired response through counter-conditioning — programming a new emotional or automatic response to the stimulus by giving it a new association. Here's how you would counter-condition a Beagle who chases after skateboarders while you're walking him on a leash.

1. Have a large supply of high-value treats, such as canned chicken.

2. Station yourself with your Beagle on a leash at a location where skateboarders will pass by at a subthreshold distance "X" — that is, where your Beagle is alerted to the approaching person but doesn't bark.

3. Wait for a skateboarder. The instant your Beagle notices the skateboarder, feed him bits of chicken, nonstop, until the skateboarder is gone. Stop feeding him.

4. Repeat many times until, when the skateboarder appears, your Beagle looks at you with a big grin as if to say, "Yay! Where's my chicken?" This is a conditioned emotional response, or CER.

5. When you have a consistent CER at distance X, decrease the distance slightly, perhaps by a foot, and repeat until you consistently get the CER at this distance.

6. Continue decreasing the distance and obtaining a CER at each level, until a skateboarder zooming right past your Beagle elicits the "Where's my chicken?" response. Now go back to distance X and add a second skateboarder. Continue this process of desensitization until your Beagle doesn't turn a nose at a bevy of skateboarders.

CHANGING

BAD BEHAVIOR

Discipline — training one to act in accordance with rules — brings order to life. It is as simple as that. Without discipline, particularly in a group society, chaos reigns supreme and the group will suffer for it. Humans and canines are social animals and need some form of discipline in order to function effectively. Dogs need discipline in their lives in order to understand how their pack (you and other family members) functions and how they must act in order to survive.

Living with an untrained Beagle is a lot like owning a piano you do not know how to play; it's a nice object to look at, but it doesn't do much more than that to bring you pleasure. Now, try taking piano lessons; suddenly the piano comes alive, bringing forth sounds and rhythms that set your heart singing and your body swaying.

The same is true of your Beagle. A dog is a big responsibility, and if your dog isn't properly trained, he may develop behaviors that annoy you or cause family friction.

Did You Know?

Anxiety can make a pup miserable. Living in a world with scary, monsters and suspected Beagle-eaters roaming the streets has to be pretty nerve-wracking. The good news is that timid dogs are not doomed to be forever ruled by fear. Owners who understand a timid Beagle's needs can help her build self-confidence and a more optimistic view of life beyond the backyard.

If your Beagle chews on shoes and other items, replace them with chewworthy toys and keep your belongings out of your pup's reach.

To train your Beagle, you can enroll in an obedience class to teach him good manners as you learn how and why he behaves the way he does. You will also find out how to communicate with your Beagle and how to recognize and understand his communications with you. Suddenly your dog takes on a new role in your life; he is interesting, smart, well behaved and fun to be with. He demonstrates his bond of devotion to you daily. In other words, your Beagle does wonders for your ego because he constantly reminds you that you are not only his leader, you are his hero!

Those involved with teaching dog obedience and counseling owners about their dogs' behavior have discovered interesting facts about dog ownership. For example, training dogs when they are puppies results in the highest success rate in developing well-mannered and well-adjusted adults. Training an older Beagle, from 6 months to

6 years, can produce almost equal results, providing the owner accepts the dog's slower learning rate and is willing to patiently work to help him succeed. Unfortunately, many owners of untrained adult dogs lack the patience, so they do not persist until their dogs are successful at learning particular behaviors.

Training a 10- to 16-week-old Beagle pup (20 weeks maximum) is like working with a dry sponge in a pool of water. The pup soaks up whatever you teach him and constantly looks for more to do and learn. At this early age, his body is not yet producing hormones, and therein lies the reason for such a high success rate. Without hormones, he is focused on you and is not particularly interested in investigating other places, dogs, people, etc.

You are his leader; his provider of food, water, shelter and security. Your Beagle latches onto you and wants to stay close.

SMART TIP!

The golden rule of dog training is simple. For each "question" (cue), there is only one correct answer (reaction). One cue equals one reaction. Keep practicing the cue until your dog reacts correctly without hesitation. Be repetitive but not monotonous. Dogs get bored just as people do; a bored dog's attention will not be focused on the lesson.

He will usually follow you from room to room, won't let you out of his sight when you are outdoors with him and will respond in like manner to the people and animals you encounter. If you greet a friend warmly, he will happily greet the person as well. If, however, you are hesitant, even anxious, about the approaching stranger, he will also respond accordingly.

Once your puppy begins to produce hormones, his natural curiosity emerges and he begins to investigate the world around him. It is at this time when you may notice your untrained dog begins to wander away and ignore your cues to stay close.

There are usually training classes within a reasonable distance of your home, but you also can do a lot to train your dog yourself. Sometimes classes are available but the tuition is too costly, whatever the circumstances, information about training your Beagle without formal obedience classes lies within the pages of this book. If the recommended procedures are followed faithfully, you can expect positive results that will prove rewarding for both you and your dog.

Whether your new Beagle is a puppy or a mature adult, the teaching methods and training techniques used in basic behaviors are the same. No dog likes harsh or inhumane training methods. All creatures, respond favorably to gentle motivational methods and sincere encouragement.

The following behavioral issues are those most commonly encountered. Remember, every dog and situation is unique. Because behavioral abnormalities are the leading reason for owners' abandoning their pets, we hope that you will make a valiant effort to solve your Beagle's behavioral issues.

Did You Know?

Dogs do not understand our language. They can be trained, however, to react to a certain sound, at a certain volume. Never use your Beagle's name during a reprimand, as she might come to associate it with a bad thing!

THE NOSE KNOWS

For every one scent receptor in the human nose, a dog has 44, for a total of 220 million compared to man's paltry 5 million. Is it any wonder then, that dogs seem so much more tuned into their environments? Now consider the Beagle. While the nose of this member of the scent hound group is built pretty much like any other dog's, centuries of selective breeding for hunting have created a breed driven by its sensitive snout. Nothing gets past a Beagle's olfactories. Nothing.

However, for all the smiles these sniffers bring, there's equal opportunity for heartbreak. The nose goes down and the rest of the world doesn't exist. You hear a lot of people say, 'Oh, I used to have a Beagle, but it got run over by a car.' Unfortunately, that happens a lot. They'll run after something, and if they're on a scent, they don't care that there's a big rig coming down the road. It doesn't even penetrate their consciousness.

Taken by the scent of a deer or rabbit or fox — or possibly a nearby fast-food restaurant — a Beagle is likely to bolt, leaving his owner to worry and fret — and hope for the best. For that reason, Beagle enthusiasts insist dogs belong on a leash when not in a fenced area. Many dog owners prefer a flexible leash that is long and expandable.

If you are out, your Beagle should never be off the leash. After all, you may have him by a leash, but you will never take away his desire to bolt after a peculiar scent. That's always going to be there because there are all these wonderful smells floating around.

Truth be told, for all the careful attention a Beagle's nose demands of his owner, there is definitely something enchanting about watching a Beagle intently follow a scent — whether he is on the field or is simply at home honing in on the smell of bacon sizzling in the frying pan.

Your Beagle may howl, whine or otherwise vocalize her displeasure at your leaving the house and her being left alone. This is a normal case of separation anxiety, but there are things that can be done to eliminate this problem. Your dog needs to learn that she will be fine on her own for a while and that she will not wither away if she isn't attended to every minute of the day.

In fact, constant attention can lead to separation anxiety in the first place. If you are endlessly coddling and cuddling your Beagle, she will come to expect this from you all of the time, and it will be more traumatic for her when you are not there.

To help minimize separation anxiety, make your entrances and exits as low-key as possible. Do not give your Beagle a long, drawn-out good-bye, and do not lavish her with hugs and kisses when you return. This will only make her miss you more when you are away. Another thing you can try is to give your dog a treat when you leave; this will keep her occupied, her mind off the fact that you just left and help her associate your leaving with a pleasant experience.

You may have to acclimate your Beagle to being left alone in intervals, much like when you introduced her to her crate. Of course, when your dog starts whimpering as you approach the door, your first instinct will be to run to her and comfort her, but don't do it! Eventually, she will adjust and be just fine — if you take it in small steps. Her anxiety stems from being placed in an unfamiliar situation; by familiarizing her with being alone, she will learn that she will be just fine. When your Beagle is alone in the house, confine her in her crate or a designated dog-proof area. This should be the area in which she sleeps, so she will already feel comfortable there and this should make her feel more at ease when she is alone. This is just one of the many examples in which a crate is an invaluable tool for you and your Beagle, and another reinforcement of why your dog should view her crate as a happy place of her own.

AT HOME WITH A NOSE

Around the house, living with a Beagle presents even more challenges. When housetraining the average pup, most owners watch for the nose to go down as a sign it's time to head outdoors.

In addition, generic puppy-proofing simply won't do. The Beagle's incredible nose means he's incredibly food-driven, and special precautions must be taken around the house to keep a Beagle out of trouble. These steps must continue throughout your dog's life and require special vigilance by the owner. For this reason, many Beagle owners crate or confine their dogs when they're not at home.

With all the trouble Beagles being so scent-driven can create, how do owners cope? It's all about channeling a Beagle's drive toward positive outlets, enthusiasts agree. Obedience is essential, as is regular exercise, whether it comes in the form of a brisk walk or a tracking trial.

Many options exist for an owner who is looking to go beyond the daily walk. For the sports-minded enthusiast, there's beagling, an age-old activity in which Beagles work in packs to hunt down small prey such as rabbits and foxes. You can find a beagling club pretty much anywhere in the country by contacting the National Beagle Club of America.

Because the breed is nonintimidating to people, the occasional Beagle nose is also employed in search-and-rescue work and contraband sniffing. If your interests lie in this direction, many books and online resources will help you get started.

Despite a reputation for being stubborn and difficult to train, with the right training methods, Beagles excel at obedience, tracking and agility — all activities that strengthen the bond between dog and owner.

BEAGLE-PROOF YOUR LIFE

For the novice and the old pro alike, living with a nose takes some thought and effort. The Beagle's sensitive snout and connected voracious appetite mean a lifetime of Beagle-proofing — in ways you may never have imagined. The following are tips for living with these perpetual curious toddlers:

■ Keep dog food and treats in air-tight, sealed containers; then put the containers behind closed doors.

■ Clear the counters and tabletops of anything edible. This includes food items from fruit to defrosting steak, as well as things you might not typically consider food. Gum, mints, cough drops and potpourri are favorites. Many Beagles are known for their counter-surfing abilities, where they jump up once to see what's there, then jump again and again until they get their prey. Even a head of lettuce may not be safe.

■ Push in table chairs or a Beagle will climb onto the table for a tasty snack.

■ Your purse isn't safe either. Whether you stash candies or sugar packets in your favorite tote, keep it safely locked away.

■ Keep trash cans behind closed doors. If you have a bin in your office, limit the contents to paper items. Take Styrofoam packing chips and other bits of cardboard out of the house because some Beagles will eat them.

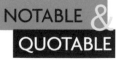

NOTABLE & QUOTABLE

Stage false departures. Pick up your car keys and put on your coat, then put them away and go about your routine. Do this several times a day, ignoring your dog while you do it. Soon, her reaction to these triggers will decrease.

— *September Morn, a dog trainer and behavior specialist in Bellingham, Wash.*

■ As with any breed, keep poisons in a locked cupboard in the garage. Also keep electrical cords out of reach a puppy's reach.

■ Watch your bathroom habits, too. You may turn your nose up at used tissue or women's sanitary items, but Beagles have been known to eat them — with dangerous consequences.

■ Pick up the soap. Some Beagles nibble on the scented varieties.

■ In the car, even the glove box isn't necessarily Beagle-proof if you aren't around to supervise. Keep your Beagle crated while in a vehicle to keep him out of trouble and your lunch safe.

NIP NIPPING

As puppies start to teethe, they feel the need to sink their teeth into anything — unfortunately that includes your fingers, arms, hair, toes, whatever happens to be available. You may find this behavior cute for the first five seconds, until you feel just how sharp those puppy teeth are.

Nipping is something you want to discourage immediately and consistently with a firm "No!" (or whatever number of firm "nos" it takes for your dog to understand that you mean business) and replace your finger with an appropriate chew toy.

STOP THAT WHINING

A puppy will often cry, whine, whimper, or howl when he is left alone. This is his way of calling out for attention and making sure that you haven't forgotten about him. He feels insecure when he is left alone; for example, when you are out of the house and he is in his crate, or when you are in another part of the house and he cannot see you.

The noise he is making is an expression of the anxiety he feels at being alone, so he

If your pup whines, don't let your frustrations get the best of you; he just wants your attention!

needs to be taught that being alone is OK. You are not actually training your Beagle to stop making noise, you are training him to feel comfortable when he is alone and thus removing the need to make the noise.

This is where his crate with a cozy blanket and a toy comes in handy. You want to know that your pup is safe when you are not there to supervise, and you know he will be in his crate rather than roaming about the house. In order for your pup to stay in his crate without making a fuss, he needs to be comfortable there. On that note, it is extremely important that the crate is never used as a form of punishment, or your Beagle puppy will have a negative association with his crate.

Accustom your puppy to his crate in short, gradually increasing time intervals. During these periods, put him in the crate, maybe with a treat, and stay in the room with him. If he cries or makes a fuss, do not go to him, but stay in his sight. Gradually, he will realize staying in his crate is all right without your help and he will not be so traumatic for him when you are not around. You may want to leave the radio on softly when you leave the house; the sound of human voices can comfort him.

CHEW ON THIS

The national canine pastime is chewing! Every dog loves to sink his "canines" into a tasty bone, but anything will do! Dogs chew to massage their gums, make their new teeth feel better and exercise their jaws. This is a natural behavior deeply embedded in all things canine. Owners should not stop their dog's chewing, but redirect it to chewworthy objects. A smart owner will purchase proper chew toys for their Beagle, like strong nylon bones. Be sure that these devices are

safe and durable because your dog's safety is at risk.

The best solution is prevention: That is, put your shoes, handbags and other alluring objects in their proper places (out of the reach of the growing canine mouth). Direct puppies to their toys whenever you see them tasting the furniture legs or the leg of your pants. Make a loud noise to attract your Beagle pup's attention and immediately escort him to his chew toy and engage him with the toy for at least four minutes, praising and encouraging him all the while.

NO MORE JUMPING

Jumping is a dog's friendly way of saying hello! Some owners don't mind when their dog jumps, which is fine for them. The problem arises when guests arrive and your dog greets them in the same manner — whether they like it or not! However friendly the greeting may be, chances are your visitors will not appreciate your dog's enthusiasm. Since he can't distinguish whom he can or cannot jump on, it is probably best to discourage this behavior entirely.

Pick a cue such as "off" (avoid using "down" because you will use that for when

Do not have long practice sessions with your Beagle. She will easily become bored if you do. Also: Never practice when you are tired, ill, worried or in a negative mood. This will transmit to your Beagle and may have an adverse effect on her performance.

you want your dog to lie down) and tell him "off" when he jumps. Place him on the ground on all fours and have him sit, praising him the whole time. Always lavish him with praise and petting when he is in the sit position, that way you are still giving him a warm, affectionate greeting, because you are as pleased to see him as he is to see you!

UNWANTED BARKING MUST GO

Barking is how dogs talk. It can be somewhat frustrating because it is not easy to tell what your dog means by his bark: Is he excited, happy, frightened, angry? Whatever it is your dog is trying to say, he should not be punished for barking. It is only when barking becomes excessive, and when excessive barking becomes a bad habit, that the behavior needs to be modified.

If an intruder came into your home in the middle of the night and your dog barked a warning, wouldn't you be pleased? You probably would deem your dog a hero, a wonderful guardian and protector of the home. On the other hand, if a friend unexpectedly drops by, rings the doorbell and is greeted with a sudden sharp bark, you probably would be annoyed at your dog. But isn't

Your dog looks to you for guidance when it comes to training, so be persistent and consistent.

it the same behavior? Your dog doesn't know any better … unless he sees who is at the door, and it is someone he is familiar with, he will bark as a means of vocalizing that his (and your) territory is being threatened. While your friend is not posing a threat, it is all the same to your dog. Barking is his means of letting you know there is an intruder, whether friend or foe, on your property. This type of barking is instinctive and should not be discouraged.

Excessive, habitual barking, however, is a problem that should be corrected early on. As your Beagle grows up, you will be able to tell when his barking is purposeful and when it is for no reason, you will able to distinguish your dog's different barks and with what they are associated. For example, the bark when someone comes to the door will be different from the bark when he is excited to see you. It is similar to a person's tone of voice, except that your Beagle has to completely rely on tone because he does not have the benefit of using words.

There are some things you might do that will encourage barking. For example, if your dog barks nonstop for a few minutes and you give him a treat to quiet him, he believes you are rewarding him for barking. He will associate barking with getting a treat and will keep barking until he receives his reward.

FOOD STEALING AND BEGGING

Is your Beagle devising ways of stealing food from your cupboards? If so, you must answer the following questions: Is your dog really hungry? Why is there food on the coffee table? Face it, some dogs are more food motivated than others; some are totally obsessed by a slab of brisket and can only think of their next meal. Food stealing is terrific fun and always yields a great reward — food, glorious food!

Therefore, the owner's goal is to make the reward less rewarding, even startling! Plant a shaker can (an empty can with a lid and filled with coins) on the table so that it catches your pooch off guard. There are other devices available that will surprise your dog when he is looking for a mid-afternoon snack. Such remote-control devices, though not the first choice of some trainers, allow the correction to come from the object instead of you. These devices are also useful to keep your snacking Beagle from napping on forbidden furniture.

Just like food stealing, begging is a favorite pastime of hungry pups with the same reward — food! Dogs learn quickly that humans love that feed-me pose and that their owners keep the good food for themselves. Why would humans dine on kibble when they can cook up sausages and kielbasa? Begging is a conditioned response related to a specific stimulus, time and place; the sounds of the kitchen, cans and bottles opening, crinkling bags and the smell of food preparation will excite your chowhound and soon his paws will be in the air!

Here is how to stop this behavior: Never give in to a beggar, no matter how appealing or desperate! By giving in, you are

NOTABLE & QUOTABLE *The purpose of puppy classes is for puppies to learn how to learn. The pups get the training along the way, but the training is almost secondary.*
— professional trainer Peggy Shunick Duezabou of Helena, Mont.

Playing with your dog and exercising him will tire him out and thwart bad behavior.

rewarding your dog for jumping up, whining and rubbing his nose into you. By ignoring your dog, you eventually will force the behavior into extinction. Note that his behavior likely gets worse before it disappears, so be sure there are not any "softies" in the family who will give in to your Beagle every time he whimpers "Please."

DIG THIS

Digging, seen as a destructive behavior by humans, is actually quite a natural behavior in dogs, though their desire to dig can be irrepressible and frustrating. When digging happens, it is an innate behavior redirected into something a dog can do in his everyday life. In the wild, a dog would be actively seeking food, making his own shelter, etc. He would be using his paws in a purposeful manner for his survival. Because you provide him with food and shelter, he has no need to use his paws for these purposes and so the energy he would be using may manifest itself in the form of holes all over your yard and flower beds.

Perhaps your dog is digging as a reaction to boredom — it is somewhat similar to someone eating a whole bag of chips in front of the TV — because they are there and there is nothing better to do! Basically, the answer is to provide your dog with adequate play and exercise so his mind and paws are occupied, and so he feels productive.

Of course, digging is easiest to control if it is stopped as soon as possible, but it is often hard to catch your dog in the act. If your Beagle is a compulsive digger and is not easily distracted by other activities, you can designate an area on your property where it is OK for him to dig. If you catch him digging in an off-limits area of the yard, immediately bring him to the approved area and praise him for digging there. Keep a close eye on him so you can catch him in the act — that is the only way to make him understand where digging is permitted and where it is not. If you take him to a hole he dug an hour ago and tell him "no," he will understand that you are not fond of holes, dirt or flowers. If you catch him while he is stifle-deep in your tulips, that is when he will get your message.

POOP ALERT!

Humans find feces eating, aka *coprophagia*, one of the most disgusting behaviors that their dog could engage in; yet to your dog it is perfectly normal. Vets have found that diets with low digestibility, containing relatively low levels of fiber and high levels of starch, increase *coprophagia*. Therefore, high-fiber diets may decrease the likelihood of your dog eating feces. To discourage this behavior, feed nutritionally complete food in the proper amount. If changes in his diet do not seem to work, and no medical cause can be found, you will have to modify his behavior through environmental control before it becomes a habit.

There are some tricks you can try, such as adding an unpleasant-tasting substance to the feces to make them unpalatable or adding something to your dog's food which will make it taste unpleasant after it passes through your dog. The best way to prevent your dog from eating his stool is to make it unavailable — clean up after he eliminates and remove any stool from the yard. If it is not there, he cannot eat it.

Never reprimand your dog for stool eating, as this rarely impresses your dog. Vets recommend distracting your Beagle while he is in the act. Another option is to muzzle your dog when he goes in the yard to relieve himself; this usually is effective within 30 to 60 days. *Coprophagia* is mostly seen in pups 6 to 12 months of age, and usually disappears around a dog's first birthday.

SEXUAL BEHAVIOR

Dogs exhibit certain sexual behaviors that may have influenced your choice of purchasing a male or female Beagle. To a certain extent, spaying/neutering will eliminate these behaviors, but if you are purchasing a dog whom you wish to breed, you should be aware of what you will have to deal with throughout your dog's life.

Female dogs usually have two estruses (heat cycle) per year with each season lasting about three weeks. These are the only times in which a female dog will mate, and she usually will not allow this until the second week of the cycle, but this does vary from female to female. If not bred during the heat cycle, it is not uncommon for a female to experience a false pregnancy, in which her mammary glands swell and she exhibits maternal tendencies toward toys or other objects.

Smart Beagle owners must also recognize that mounting is not merely a sexual expression; it is also one of dominance and is usually exhibited when dogs meet for the first time, and they must negotiate their place in the canine heirarchy. Be consistent in your training, and you will find that you can move a mounter.

FOR THE FUN

One of the best ways to nurture a cooperative and solid relationship with your Beagle is to become involved in an activity.

Deciding what recreation you and your Beagle would enjoy the most takes some consideration. Do you want a sport, such as agility, where you and your dog are both active participants? Would you prefer an activity, such as flyball, where your dog does most of the running? Does something less physical, such as visiting senior citizens, sound more like your cup of tea? Perhaps a brief synopsis of some of the more popular dog-friendly recreational sports will help you narrow down the choices.

EXERCISE OPTIONS

All Beagles need exercise to keep them physically and mentally healthy. An inactive hound will become an inflated hound, who will likely suffer joint strain or torn ligaments from the extra weight. Inactive dogs also are prone to mischief and may do anything to relieve their boredom. This often leads to behavioral problems, such as chewing or barking. Regular daily exercise, such as walks and play sessions, will keep your Beagle slim, trim and happy.

Provide your Beagle with interactive play that stimulates his mind as well as his body.

Did You Know? The Fédération Internationale Cynologique is the world kennel club that governs dog shows in Europe and elsewhere around the world.

Before You Begin
Because of the physical demands of sporting activities, a Beagle puppy shouldn't begin official training until she is done growing. That doesn't mean, though, that you can't begin socializing her to sports. Talk to your veterinarian about what age is appropriate to begin.

It's a good idea to have a daily period of one-on-one play, especially with a puppy or young dog. Continue this type of interaction throughout your dog's life, and you will build a lasting bond. Even senior Beagles need the stimulation that activity provides.

If your Beagle is older or overweight, consult your veterinarian about how much and what type of exercise he needs. Usually, a 10- to 15-minute walk once a day is a good start. As the pounds start to drop off, your dog's energy level will rise, and you can increase the amount of daily exercise.

Whether a dog is trained in the structured environment of a class or alone with his owner at home, there are many sporting activities that can bring fun and rewards to the owner and his dog once they have achieved basic control.

SCENT HURDLES

Scenting — a natural for those amazing noses. This can be fun with only your Beagle as a partner or as a team sport. Dogs must jump hurdles to reach a platform with objects on top, such as dumbbells, in competition. Finding the object with the scent of the owner is bit-time fun for Beagles. Teams have timed events with one dog quickly leaping into action as soon as the prior one returns with the object in his mouth and yields it to his handler.

The most difficult part of this event is to restrain the highly excited dogs until it

Having your Beagle participate in canine activities boosts his confidence and gives him a sense of purpose.

becomes their turn. If a hurdle is missed or the wrong dumbbell is selected, the dog must go to the end and run again. In competition, the hurdles are set to accommodate the smallest dog on the team. Hurdles are placed 10 feet apart with the platform 12 feet beyond the last hurdle.

TRACKING

Beagles excel at tracking because, once again, they are able to use their extraordinary sense of smell. A track is laid and allowed to age. The dog is permitted to fill his nose and brain with the scent of the tracklayer. Then he is asked to follow it through hills and valleys, twists and turns, possibly across different surfaces according to the difficulty of the track. Objects are planted for the dog to detect at various points along the way.

Carole Bolan of Groton, Mass., has put American and Canadian tracking titles on eight Beagles. But, she says, "It's too dangerous to let dogs run loose any more. With tracking, we allow them to use their natural abilities in a controlled situation." Instead of running off-leash, they are allowed 20 feet of freedom with a long tracking leash.

"Beagles have a specific wag when they scent a rabbit, so I've learned to read their tails," Bolan says. "One of mine tracked from the field into the woods and her tail began to signal the bunny scent. So I gave her the command to get back on track. The farther into a track they go, the more intent they become."

Some owners participate in more than one field of competition, and the breed boasts a few dual champion Beagles in bench and field. The official rules state, "The Beagle is a trailing hound whose purpose is to find game, to pursue it in an energetic and decisive manner, and to show determination to account for it."

Although many people trial Beagles individually, others participate in Brace, Small Packs, Large Packs or Small Pack Option. Hounds are measured to run in 13-inch or 15-inch packs or braces, which involves two dogs running together. SPO is run in packs of five to nine, in which the dogs flat-out run, says Brenda Hulsey of Evansville, Ind., secretary, treasurer and field trial secretary of the Tri State Beagle Club based in Haubstadt. "They are very fast," she says. "This is a young person's sport because only the young can keep up with the dogs."

Beagles do well in pack situations because they're sociable and friendly with other dogs. As many as 50 Beagles may participate in a Large Pack trial, which are run on a larger hare. When a hound is faulty in the run, it is eliminated. The winners of each SPO compete in a winners' pack.

During a trial, the judges, handlers and gallery can walk along to watch the hounds work in a Brace, or occasionally a trio if the entry is large. People beat the brush trying to flush a cottontail. When one is sighted, the cry of "tallyho" is sounded and the point marked with a tallyho stick.

NOTABLE & QUOTABLE

When my Beagles did something right for me, I'd reward them with a hug, pet them, talk to them and really love 'em up. That seemed to work well, especially since they're very loving, family-oriented, snuggly dogs.

— Beagle owner Judy Watts from Santa Ana, Calif.

At that time, the dogs are put "on the line." The dogs must pick up the scent and bark, and they are then let off-leash to track. Hounds must follow the scent and give voice at each place the rabbit stops. No one wants their Beagle to see the bunny and break into a sight chase. Any hound that begins to run is eliminated.

A similar noncompetitive situation can be created simply by walking your Beagle through woods or pastures, watching him pick up the scent of a small animal, such as a rabbit, and following the trail. "Beaglers" — Beagle owners who compete in field trials with their dogs — say hearing the breed give voice, or tongue, when finding its quarry is a thrilling moment.

AGILITY TRIALS

Agility is a fast-growing sport, attracting dogs of all kinds and their equally diverse owners. In agility, the dog — off leash but guided by the handler — runs a course of obstacles including jumps, tunnels, A-frames, elevated boards called dog walks and others. Basically, the dog must navigate through the obstacles in proper order and style within a set time. As in obedience, the team can strive for high honors, the titles only or simply the joy of working together.

Most training facilities require dogs to have some basic obedience before entering an agility class because your dog must be responsive to you and reliable about not interfering with other dogs and handlers or running off. Allow your puppy to mature before undertaking agility's jumps and sharp turns because young bones and joints are injured more easily than mature ones.

Multiple organizations sponsor agility titles at all levels, from novice to advanced. The rules, procedures and obstacles vary somewhat among the organizations, so,

again, it's important to obtain and read the appropriate rule book before entering your dog in competition. In addition to the American Kennel Club, the United Kennel Club, the United States Dog Agility Association and the North American Dog Agility Council also offer agility trials and canine titles.

The AKC offers Novice Agility, Open Agility, Agility Excellent and Master Agility Excellent titles. To achieve an MX title, a dog must first earn the AX title, then earn qualifying scores in the agility excellent class at 10 licensed or member agility trials.

The USDAA offers eight agility titles. An Agility Dog has achieved three clear rounds (no faults) under two different judges in the starters or novice category of the competition. An Advanced Agility Dog has achieved three clear rounds under two different judges in the Advanced class. The Masters Agility Dog has demonstrated versatility by achieving three clear rounds under two different judges in the masters standard agility class.

In addition, a dog must receive a qualifying score at the masters level in each of the following: Gamblers Competition, to demonstrate a dog's proficiency in distance control and handling; Pairs or Team Relay, to demonstrate a dog's sportsmanship and his ability to work well in a team; Jumping Class, to demonstrate his jumping ability and fluid, controlled working habit; and Snooker Competition, to further demonstrate a dog and handler's versatility, proficiency and cooperation in strategic planning.

To earn a Jumpers Master, Gamblers Master, Snooker Master or Relay Master title, a dog must achieve five clear rounds in the appropriate class. A USDAA Agility Dog Champion has earned the MAD, SM, GM, JM and RM titles. The USDAA also recognizes the Agility Top 10 annually.

USDAA hosts major tournament events, including its Grand Prix of Dog Agility championships. The Dog Agility Masters Team Pentathlon Championship promotes agility as a team sport, and the Dog Agility Steeplechase championship focuses on speed performance. Dogs must be registered with the USDAA in order to compete.

The USDAA also offers programs for older dogs and younger handlers. The Veterans Program is for dogs 7 years of age or older. The Junior Handler Program is for handlers up to 18 years of age and is designed to encourage young people to participate in dog agility as a fun, recreational family sport.

The North American Dog Agility Council offers Certificates of Achievement for the regular jumpers and gamblers classes. The purpose of the regular agility class is to demonstrate the handler and dog's ability to perform all of the agility obstacles safely and at a moderate rate of speed. At the open level, the goal is to test the handler and dog's ability to perform the obstacles more quickly and with more directional and distance control and obstacle discrimination.

At the elite level, more complex handler strategies are tested, with the dog moving briskly. The dog may be entered in the standard, veterans or junior handlers division. In

Agility has plenty of fun obstacles — from jumps to tunnels to turns to hoops — that are sure to keep your Beagle enthused.

all divisions, certification in the regular agility classes will require three qualifying rounds under at least two different judges. NADAC also awards the Agility Trial Champion title.

OBEDIENCE TRIALS

Obedience trials in the United States trace back to the early 1930s, when organized obedience training was developed to demonstrate how well dogs and their owners could work together. Helen Whitehouse Walke, a Standard Poodle fancier, pioneered obedience trials after she modeled a series of exercises after the Associated Sheep, Police and Army Dog Society of Great Britain. Since Walker initiated the first trials, competitive obedience has grown by leaps and bounds, and today more than 2,000 trials are held in the United States every year, with more than 100,000 dogs competing. Any registered AKC or UKC dog can enter an obedience trial for the club in which he is registered, regardless of conformational disqualifications or neutering.

Obedience trials are divided into three levels of progressive difficulty. At the first level, Novice, the dogs compete for the title of Companion Dog; at the intermediate level, Open, dogs compete for a Companion Dog Excellent title; and at the Advanced level, dogs compete for a Utility Dog title. Classes are subdivided into "A" (for beginners) and "B" (for more experienced handlers). A perfect score at any level is 200, and a dog must score 170 or better to earn a "leg," of which three are needed to earn the title. To earn points, the dog must score more than 50 percent of the available points in each exercise; the possible points range from 20 to 40.

Once a dog has earned the Utility Dog title, he can compete with other proven obedience dogs for the coveted title of Utility Dog Excellent, which requires that the dog win "legs" in 10 shows. In 1977, the title Obedience Trial Champion was established by the AKC. Utility Dogs who earn legs in Open B and Utility B earn points toward their Obedience Trial Champion title. To become an OTCh., a dog needs to earn 100 points, which requires three first place wins in Open B and Utility under three different judges.

The Grand Prix of obedience trials, the AKC National Obedience Invitational, gives qualifying Utility Dogs the chance to win the newest and highest title: National Obedience Champion. Only the top 25 ranked obedience dogs, plus any dog ranked in the top three in his breed, are allowed to compete.

RALLY BEHIND RALLY

Rally is a sport that combines competition obedience with elements of agility, but is less demanding than either one of these activities. Rally was designed keeping the average dog owner in mind, and is easier than many other sporting activities.

At a rally event, dogs and handlers are asked to move through 10 to 20 different stations that are marked by numbered signs, which tell the handler the exercise to be performed. The exercises vary from making different types of turns to changing pace.

If you find your Beagle isn't suited for group activities, once you get your veterinarian's OK and basic obedience training behind you, you and your Beagle can find plenty of opportunities for exercise, training and strengthening the bond between you, right in your own backyard.

SMART TIP!

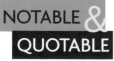

NOTABLE & QUOTABLE

The scent drive is so strong in this breed that they need to stay on the leash for a longer time. For example, when heeling, they tend to keep their noses to the ground. They do not focus on you.

— dog trainer Caryl Crouse of Canine Miss Manners in Walpole, Mass.

Teaching your Beagle to watch your every move begins when you first bring her home. Puppies will automatically follow you, even without a leash, because they want to be with you, especially if you have a treat in your hand. Keep your dog on your left side and offer her a small piece of food with each step you take. In no time, your Beagle pup will think that you're an automatic treat dispenser, and she will never leave your side.

Dogs can earn rally titles as they get better at the sport and move through the different levels. The titles to strive for are Rally Novice, Rally Advanced, Rally Excellent and Rally Advanced Excellent.

To get your puppy prepared to enter a rally competition, focus on teaching him basic obedience, for starters. Your dog must know the five basic obedience cues — sit, lie down, stay, come and heel — and perform them well. Next, you can enroll your dog in a rally class. Although he must be at least 6 months of age to compete in rally, you can start training long before his 6-month birthday.

FLYBALL

Fast and intense, flyball consists of four consecutive hurdles set at a height appropriate for the shortest dog on the team. Just beyond the hurdles sits every dog's dream machine — a spring-loaded box that ejects a tennis ball at the push of a pedal. For competition, each member of the four-dog team must leap the hurdles, jump on the release pedal, catch the ball and repeat his path back to the waiting handler, allowing the next dog to begin.

A sport that revolves around catching and carrying tennis balls while racing other dogs promises tremendous fun for Beagles, often prompting them to voice their excitement with joyful barks and howls.

Obviously, with racing, jumping and impacting a stationary object, the Beagle's physique warrants a few concerns, particularly when "hitting" the box.

Approached with common sense, flyball represents a great pursuit for dog and handler. Less common than agility, flyball classes can be difficult to find. Ask fellow trainers if they know of anyone active in flyball willing to work with a newcomer. Another option is to contact the North American Flyball Association, the ruling organization that bestows flyball titles and maintains breed statistics, for information on a local club or, if necessary, how to start one yourself.

MUSICAL FREESTYLE

A stunning combination of obedience, tricks and dance, freestyle is the perfect venue for those possessing an artistic flair. Set within a large, open ring, each handler and dog pair perform a personally choreographed routine in rhythm to their choice of music. A typical presentation might find a dog weaving between the handler's legs as he or she is walking, spinning in place, doing leg kicks and other imaginative moves. Creative handler costumes and fancy dog collars often complete the picture.

Most participants agree that dogs display preferences in music, responding happily to tunes they like while ignoring those they don't. Debora Wheeler of Gilmanton, N.H., says her Beagle, Cain, greatly enjoys freestyle training. "He's a happy little dog who loves to perform," she says.

Let the Games Begin!

When you've tired of playing hound games with just you and your dog, plan the following series of Beagle games for your next club picnic or party.

Musical Mats: A doggie version of musical chairs, place small mats or paper plates in a circle with one less than the total number of players. Have owners line up with their Beagles. When the music ends, dogs dart for the nearest mat and sit on it. If the Beagle doesn't sit, the owner must. The one without a mat is cut from the circle and one mat is removed. Last Beagle — or Beagle owner with Beagle in hand — on a mat wins.

Hog Dog: Arrange a plate full of unusual goodies for each Beagle: cauliflower, broccoli, slice of banana, strawberry, melon, pickle, or anything healthy that is not normal dog food or treats. The leader calls out the name of one of the items. The Beagles who eat the specified item remain in competition. In case of a tie, the one with the least hesitation wins.

Ball Relay: Beagles walk beside their owners who balance a ball on a paper cup. Their objective is to complete their part of the relay, such as walking to a certain point and back, "tagging" the next person on the team. If the owner drops the ball, the Beagle must pick it up and give it to the owner. The fastest team wins.

Cookie Catch: First walk a foot away from your dog and toss a treat to him. Then move backward a foot at a time, tossing a treat each time you stop. A Beagle who drops or fumbles a treat is eliminated.

Hot Dog Retrieve: This game is almost impossible to complete for eternally hungry Beagles who have supernatural powers of scent. To them, hot dogs smell like a gourmet dinner. Handlers throw the tempting morsel while the Beagle is on a sit/stay. The dog is then sent on the retrieve, and the one with the most hot dog left at the return wins. This can also be done on-leash.

12-Legged Race: This is the old sack race, except with two people and two dogs, which equals 12 legs once you tie the handlers' adjacent legs together. The handlers must run to the finish line with their Beagles on-leash. It's even funnier if you have someone at the opposite end waving a cookie and calling the dogs.

Sports are physically demanding. Have your vet perform a full examination of your Beagle to rule out joint problems, heart disease, eye ailments and other maladies. Once you get the green light, start having fun in your new dog-sporting life!

If you're worried about your own questionable dance skills, keep in mind that the self-choreography allows you to focus on your team's special talents.

Find the ham in your little Beagle at a local training facility or private trainer. Alternatively, contact the sport's host organizations, the Canine Freestyle Federation and the World Canine Freestyle Organization for information about getting your start in this exciting activity.

SHOW DOGS

When you purchase your puppy, you must make it clear to the breeder whether you want one just as a lovable companion and pet, or if you hope to purchase a Beagle with show prospects. No reputable breeder will sell you a puppy and tell you that he will definitely be show quality because so much can go wrong during the early months of a puppy's development. If you do plan to show, what you hopefully will have acquired is a puppy with show potential.

To the novice, exhibiting a Beagle in the ring may look easy, but it takes a lot of hard work and devotion to win at a show such as the annual Westminster Kennel Club Dog Show in New York City, not to mention a fair amount of luck, too!

The first concept that the canine novice learns when watching a dog show is that each dog first competes against members of his own breed. Once the judge has selected the best dog in each breed (Best of Breed) the chosen dog will compete with other dogs in his group. Finally, the dogs chosen first in each group will compete for the Best In Show title.

The second concept is that the dogs are not actually compared against one another. The judge compares each dog against the breed standard, the written description of the ideal dog approved by the AKC. While some early breed standards were indeed based on specific dogs who were famous or popular, many dedicated enthusiasts say that a perfect specimen as described in the standard has never walked into a show ring, has never been bred and, to the woe of dog breeders around the globe, does not exist. Breeders attempt to get as close to this ideal as possible with every litter, but theoretically the "perfect" dog is so elusive that it is impossible. (And if the perfect dog were born, breeders and judges probably would never agree that he was perfect!)

If you are interested in exploring the world of conformation, your best bet is to join your local breed club or the national (parent) club, the National Beagle Club of America. These clubs often host regional and national specialties, shows only for Beagles, which can include conformation as well as obedience and field trials. Even if you have no intention of competing with your Beagle, a specialty is like a festival for lovers of the breed who congregate to share their favorite topic: Beagles! Clubs also send out newsletters, and some organize training days and seminars providing owners the opportunity to learn more about their chosen breed. To locate the breed club closest to you, contact the AKC, which furnishes the rules and regulations for all of these events, plus general dog registration and other basic requirements of dog ownership.

CANINE GOOD CITIZEN

If obedience work sounds too regimented but you'd still like your Beagle to have a title, prepare him for the Canine Good Citizen test. This program is sponsored by the AKC, with tests administered by local dog clubs, private trainers and 4-H clubs.

To earn a CGC title, your Beagle must be well groomed and demonstrate the manners that all good dogs should exhibit. The CGC test requires a dog to obey the sit, lie down, stay and come cues, react appropriately to other dogs and distractions, allow a stranger to approach him, sit politely for petting, walk nicely on a loose leash, move through a crowd without going wild, calm down after play or praise, and sit still for an examination by the judge.

THERAPY

Visiting nursing homes, people in hospice and hospitals with your dog can be a tremendously satisfying experience. Many times, a dog can reach out to an individual who has withdrawn from the world. The people-oriented Beagle can be a delightful therapy dog. This breed seems to have an affinity for children that makes it a natural for visiting children in hospitals or mental care facilities. Although a gentle disposition is definitely a plus, the often normally rambunctious dog seems to instinctively become gentler when introduced to those who are weak or ailing. Some basic obedience is, of course, a necessity for the therapy dog and a repertoire of tricks is a definite bonus. The sight of a clownish Beagle "hamming it up" can help brighten most anyone's day.

Most facilities require a dog to have certification from a therapy dog organization. Therapy Dog International and the Delta Society are two such organizations. Generally speaking, if your dog can pass a Canine Good Citizen test, earning certification will not be difficult. Certified therapy dog workers frequently get together in a group and regularly make visitations around hospitals in their area.

Sound the trumpets! Beagles were made for fun in the field.

RESOURCES

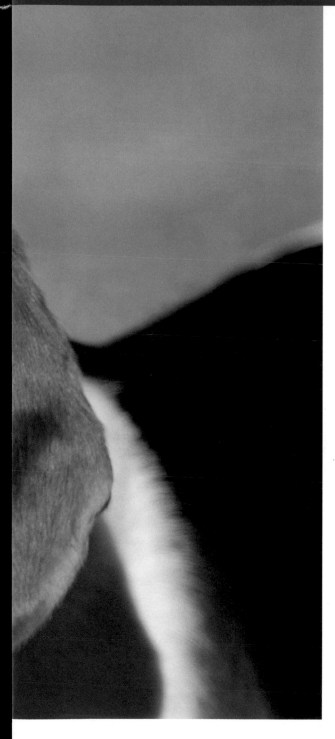

Smart owners can find out more information about this popular and fascinating breed by contacting the following organizations. They will be glad to help you dig deeper into the world of Beagles, and you won't even have to beg!

American Kennel Club: The AKC website offers information and links to conformation, tracking, rally, obedience and agility programs; member clubs; and all things dog. www.akc.org

Canadian Kennel Club: Our northern neighbor's oldest kennel club is similar to the AKC in the states. www.ckc.ca

Canine Performance Events: Sports for dogs to keep them active. www.k9cpe.com

Delta Society: This organization offers animal assistance. www.deltasociety.org

Dog Scouts of America: Take your dog to camp! www.dogscouts.com

i-barc: It's the Internet Beagle Aficionado Recreation Club. www.crackpot.org/ibarc

National Beagle Club of America: This is the national parent club of the American Kennel Club. http://clubs.akc.org/NBC

it's a **Fact**

The **American Kennel Club** was established in 1884. It is America's oldest kennel club. The AKC recognized the Beagle in 1885. The **United Kennel Club** is the second oldest in the United States and began registering dogs in 1898.

Love on a Leash: Your Beagle has a lot of love to give. www.loveonaleash.org

National Animal Poison Control Center: This website could save your dog's life! www.napcc.aspca.org

National Association of Professional Pet Sitters: Hire someone to watch your dog when you have to leave town. www.petsitters.org

North American Dog Agility Council: This site provides links to clubs, obedience trainers and agility trainers in the United States and Canada. www.nadac.com

SOS Beagle Rescue: This nonprofit finds homes for rescued Beagles. www.sosbeagles.org

Therapy Dogs Inc.: Get your Beagle involved in therapy. www.therapydogs.com

Therapy Dogs International: You can find more therapy dog information here: www.tdi-dog.org

United Kennel Club: The UKC offers several of the events offered by the AKC, including agility, conformation and obedience. In addition, the UKC offers competitions in hunting and dog sports (companion and protective events). Both the UKC and the AKC offer programs for junior handlers, ages 2 to 18. www.ukcdogs.com

United States Dog Agility Association: The USDAA has information on training, clubs and events in the United States, Canada, Mexico and overseas. www.usdaa.com

World Canine Freestyle Organization: Dancing with your dog is fun! www.worldcaninefreestyle.org

Don't let your Beagle sit around all day. Get involved in a dog sport.

Plan your vacation to include your dog. However, if your destination isn't Fido-friendly, have a good boarding place already lined up.

BOARDING

So you want to take a family vacation, and you want to include all members of the family. You usually make arrangements for accommodations ahead of time anyway, but this is imperative when traveling with a dog. You do not want to make an overnight stop at the only place around for miles only to discover that the hotel doesn't allow dogs. Also, you don't want to reserve a room for your family without confirming that you are traveling with a Beagle because if it is against the hotel's policy, you may not have a place to stay.

Alternatively, if you are traveling and choose not to bring your Beagle, you will have to make arrangements for him. Some

options are to leave him or with a reliable family member or a neighbor, have a trusted friend stop by often or stay at your house. Another option is leaving your Beagle at a reputable boarding kennel.

If you choose to board him at a kennel, visit in advance to see the facilities and check how clean they are and where the dogs are kept. Talk to some of the employees and see how they treat the dogs. Do they spend time with the dogs either during play or exercise? Find out the kennel's policy on vaccinations and what they require. This is for all of the dogs' safety because when dogs are kept together, there is a greater risk of diseases being passed between them.

HOME STAFFING

For the Beagle parent who works all day, a pet sitter or dog walker may be the perfect solution for the lonely Beagle longing for a midday stroll. Dog owners can approach local high schools or community centers if they don't have a neighbor who is interested in a part-time commitment.

When you interview potential dog walkers, consider their experience with dogs, as well as your Beagle's rapport with the candidate. (Beagles are excellent judges of character.) You should always cross-check a candidate's references before entrusting your dog to a new dog walker and opening your home to him or her.

For an owner's long-term absence, such as a business trip or vacation, many Beagle owners welcome the services of a pet sitter. It's usually less stressful on the dog to stay home with a pet sitter than to be boarded in a kennel. Pet sitters may be more affordable than a week's stay at a full-service doggie day care.

Pet sitters must be even more reliable than dog walkers because the dog is depending on his surrogate owner for all of his needs over an extended period. Owners are advised to hire a certified pet sitter through the National Association of Professional Pet Sitters (www.petsitters.org). NAPPS provides online and toll-free pet sitter

If your dog is alone all day, consider hiring a dog walker or pet sitter to keep him company.

locator services. The nonprofit organization only certifies serious-minded, professional individuals who are knowledgeable in canine behavior, nutrition, health and safety.

Whether or not you take your Beagle on a vacation with you, always keep your Beagle's best interest at heart when planning a family vacation.

SCHOOL'S IN SESSION

Puppy kindergarten, which is usually open to dogs between 3 to 6 months of age, allows puppies to learn and socialize with other dogs and people in a structured setting. Classes helps to socialize your Beagle so that he will enjoy going places with you and be a well-behaved dog in public gatherings. They prepare him for adult obedience classes and for a lifetime of social experiences he will have with your friends and his furry friends. The problem with most puppy kindergarten classes is that most are only held one night a week.

If you're home during the day, you may be able to find places to take your puppy so he can socialize. Just be careful about dog parks and other places that are open to any dog. An experience with a dog bully can undo all the good your training classes have done.

If you work, your puppy may be home alone all day, a tough situation for a Beagle. Chances are he can't hold himself that long, so your potty training will be under-mined — unless you're teaching him to use an indoor potty. Also, by the time you come home, he'll be bursting with energy, and you may think that he's hyperactive and uncontrollable.

The only suitable answer for the working professional with a Beagle is doggie day care. Most large cities have some sort of day care, whether it's a boarding kennel that keeps your dog in a run or a full-service day care that offers training, play time and even spa facilities. They range from a person who keeps a few dogs at his or her home to a

state-of-the-art facility built just for dogs. Many of the more sophisticated doggie day cares offer webcams so you can see what your dog is up to throughout the day. Things to look for:

- escape-proof facilities, such as gates in doorways that lead outside
- inoculation requirements for new dogs
- midday meals for young dogs
- obedience training (if offered), using reward-based methods
- safe and comfortable nap areas
- screening of dogs for aggression
- small groups of similar sizes and ages
- toys and playground equipment, such as tunnels and chutes
- trained staff, with an adequate number to supervise the dogs (no more than 10 to 15 dogs per person)
- a webcam

Remember to keep your dog's leash slack when interacting with other dogs. It is not unusual for a dog to pick out one or two canine neighbors to dislike. If you know there's bad blood, step off to the side and find a barrier, such as a parked car, between the dogs. If there are no barriers to be had, move to the side of the walkway, cue your Beagle to sit, stay and watch you until her nemesis passes; then continue your walk.

CAR TRAVEL

You should accustom your Beagle to riding in a car at an early age. You may or may not take him in the car often, but at the very least he will need to go to the vet once in a while, and you do not want these trips to be traumatic for your dog or troublesome for you. The safest way for a dog to ride in the car is in his crate. If he uses a crate in the house, you can use the same crate for travel.

Another option is purchasing a specially designed safety harness for dogs, which straps your Beagle in the car much like a seat belt would. Do not let your dog roam loose in the vehicle; this is very dangerous! If you should make an abrupt stop, your dog

If you take your dog for car rides, buckle him up with a dog safety harness! He's precious cargo, too!

can be thrown and injured. If your dog starts climbing on you while you are driving, you will not be able to concentrate on the road. It is an unsafe situation for everyone — human and canine.

For long trips, stop often to let your Beagle relieve himself. Take along whatever you need to clean up after him, including some paper towel should he have an accident in the car or suffer from motion sickness.

IDENTIFICATION

Your Beagle is your valued companion and friend. That is why you always keep a close eye on him, and you've made sure that he cannot escape from the yard or wriggle out of his collar and run away from you. However, accidents can happen and there may come a time when your Beagle unexpectedly gets separated from you. If this should occur, the first thing on your mind will be finding him. Proper identification, including an ID tag, a tattoo and possibly a microchip, will increase the chances of his being returned to you safely and quickly.

An ID tag on a collar or harness is the primary means of identifying a lost pet (and ID licenses are required in many cities). Although inexpensive and easy to read, collars and ID tags can come off or be taken off.

A microchip doesn't get lost. The microchip is embedded underneath the dog's skin and contains a unique ID number that is read by scanners. It comes in handy for identifying lost or stolen pets. However, to be effective, the microchip must be registered in a national database. Smart owners will register their dog as soon as he is chipped and regularly check that their contact information is kept up-to-date.

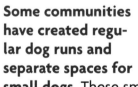

However, one thing to keep in mind is that not every shelter or veterinary clinic has a scanner, nor do most folks who might pick up and try to return a lost pet. Your best best? Get both!

INDEX

INDEX

BEAGLE, a Smart Owner's Guide™
part of the Kennel Club Books® Interactive Series™

JOIN
Club
Beagle™
TODAY!

LIBRARY OF CONGRESS CATALOGING-IN-PUBLICATION DATA

Beagle / from the editors of Dog fancy magazine.
    p. cm. — (Smart owner's guide)
Includes index and bibliography.
ISBN 978-1-59378-772-1
1. Beagle (Dog breed) I. Dog fancy (San Juan Capistrano, Calif.)
SF429.B3B43 2010
636.753′7—dc22

        2009040983